Greek and Roman MYTHOLOGY

Greek and Roman
MYTHOLOGY

D.M. Field

Hamlyn

London·New York·Sydney·Toronto

Acknowledgments

Title page:
Heracles forcing Nereus (here rather comically identified by a fish) to tell him how to find the garden of the Hesperides.

Endpapers:
The Greeks usually endowed rivers with spirits or gods of their own. Here is the god Peneus, of the river of that name, with his daughter Daphne who was one of the loves of Apollo. Roman mosaic from Cyprus.

Colour
Archivio Fratelli Fabbri Editori, Milan 106, 171; British Museum, London 91 bottom; Casa Editrice Unedi SpA, Milan 94 bottom, 96; Explorer, Paris: J-H Lelièvre 36; Werner Forman Archive, London 147 top, 156 right, 157 bottom, 174; Photographie Giraudon, Paris 157 top, 159 bottom; Lauros-Giraudon 99 top; Sonia Halliday Photographs, England endpapers, 18, 39, 51 bottom, 55, 63, 66, 72 top, 73, 84 bottom, 99 bottom, 108, 135, 142, 144 left, 154 top, 154 bottom right, 156 left, 159 top, 169, 186 bottom; Sonia Halliday Photographs: F H C Birch 24, 25; Hamlyn Group Picture Library title spread, 22, 51 top, 70, 84 top, 85, 91 top, 111 top, 115, 133 top, 154 bottom left, 187 right; Hannibal, Athens, Greece, 42, 43, 49 top, 49 bottom, 118; Hirmer Fotoarchiv, Munich 78, 97, 103, 120, 123 left; Larousse, Paris 82; The Metropolitan Museum of Art, New York 87; Pictor International Limited, London 48, 127; Scala, Antella 163, 166; Rev R V Schoder, USA 145; Michael Stapleton, London 19 top, 46, 58, 60 top, 72 bottom, 79, 121, 144 right; Tony Stone Associates, London 10, 13, 15 left, 27; University of London, The Warburg Institute 187 left; ZEFA, London: P Colton 54; Konrad Helbig 7, 31, 37, 60 bottom, 123 right, 130 right; Jürgen Kuhnke 67; Scholz 12; J Schörken 30; Starfoto 147 bottom; Studio Benser 15 right.

Black and White
Alinari, Florence 9 bottom left, 104, 167, 180, 181, 183; Almasy, Paris 8; American Academy, Rome 160 top right, 165 right, 177 left; Archives Photographiques, Paris 23 top; Ashmolean Museum, Oxford 41 bottom, 88 left, 90 left; Bibliothèque Nationale, Paris 41 top; Bildarchiv Foto Marburg 9 bottom right, 19 centre, 28 top left, 28 bottom; Phot. Boissonas, Geneva 119 top; Boudot-Lamotte, Paris 11 top, 17; British Museum, London 28 top right, 47 bottom, 53 bottom, 57 bottom, 61, 62 left, 64 bottom left, 71 top left, 77, 81 top left, 83 bottom, 88 top right, 90 right, 92, 93 top, 95 bottom, 117 top, 117 bottom, 131 right, 136; Deutsches Archäologisches Institut, Athens 59 right, 94 left; Fitzwilliam Museum, Cambridge 152 bottom; Werner Forman Archive, London 173 bottom, 178, 179; Photographie Giraudon, Paris 98, 128 top, 134 left, 161 top, 182, 188 right; Alinari-Giraudon 74 right, 107, 155 right; Anderson-Giraudon 50, 93 bottom left; Lauros-Giraudon 89 top left; Guildhall Museum, London 189; Hachette, Paris 160 top left; Sonia Halliday Photographs, England 146; Hamlyn Group Picture Library 26 bottom, 86 top, 86 bottom right, 100 top, 140, 141 top, 177 right; Photo Hassia, Paris 11 bottom; Hermitage Museum, Leningrad 93 bottom right; Hirmer Fotoarchiv, Munich 11 centre, 19 bottom, 23 bottom, 26 top, 26 centre, 29 bottom, 45 left, 47 top, 52 right, 57 top, 65, 68 left, 71 top right, 76 top, 83 right, 112 top, 113 right, 126; Kunsthistorisches Museum, Vienna 125 bottom; Larousse, Paris 29 top, 125 top; The Mansell Collection, London 32 left, 32 right, 33, 40 top, 40 bottom, 56, 59 left, 64 top, 64 bottom right, 68 right, 69 left, 71 bottom, 81 top right, 81 bottom, 86 bottom left, 89 right, 105, 112 bottom, 114 right, 116, 124 top, 128 bottom, 129, 131, 133 bottom left, 133 bottom right, 137 top, 137 bottom, 138, 141 bottom, 143, 148, 150, 152 top, 153, 155 left, 158 left, 158 right, 161 bottom, 162, 164, 165 left, 168, 170, 172, 173 top, 184, 185 left, 185 right, 186 top, 188 left; The Metropolitan Museum of Art, New York 38 top, 111, 113 left, 149; Museum für Kunst und Gewerbe, Hamburg 45 right; Museum of Fine Arts, Boston 52 left, 53 top, 62 right, 69, 80, 101, 130 left, 134 right; The National Museum, Denmark 119 bottom; Josephine Powell, Rome 16; République Arabe Syrienne, Ministère de la Culture du Tourisme et de l'Orientation Nationale 35; Roger-Viollet, Paris 14, 20, 21 bottom; Staatliche Antikensammlung und Glyptothek, Munich 38 bottom, 124 bottom; Staatliche Museen Antiken-Abteilung, Berlin 100 bottom, 122 bottom, 160 bottom; Soperintendenza alle Antichità, Florence 109, 122 top; Soperintendenza alle Antichità della Campania, Naples 88 bottom right, 95 top, 114 left; ZEFA, London 74 left; Ziolo-Held, Paris 76 bottom.

Published by
The Hamlyn Publishing Group Limited
London · New York · Sydney · Toronto
Astronaut House, Hounslow Road
Feltham, Middlesex

© Copyright The Hamlyn Publishing Group Limited 1977

ISBN 0 600 36247 7

Phototypeset in Great Britain by
Filmtype Services Limited, Scarborough

Printed in Great Britain
by Jarrold and Sons Limited, Norwich

Contents

Introduction

Not much more than one hundred years ago, the central subjects of traditional education in the West were the classics–Greek and Latin. Today 'a classical education' is a thing of the past, as out of date as the Grand Tour or the White Man's Burden. Except for that small number actually studying the classics, the majority of university students today–even those at the older universities like Oxford and Cambridge, or Harvard and Yale–do not know a word of Latin or Greek. This is an inevitable result of the growth of other disciplines– in a word the sciences, both 'hard' (mathematics, physics, etc.) and 'soft' (sociology)–over the past hundred years or so. No one, except for a few tough old reactionaries, would suggest that the educational clock should be put back, and modern students return to parsing Ovid.

The retreat of the classics means, unfortunately, that not only are we becoming relatively ignorant of the affairs of our cultural ancestors in ancient Greece and Rome, but also that we are in danger of losing touch with our own more recent culture. Virtually every writer up to the late 19th century assumed that his or her readers would be acquainted with the classics. Shakespeare set several of his finest plays in classical times, and in any of his other plays, the spectator ignorant of Greece and Rome would find many references puzzling. No one can get very far in studying English literature without at least a rough knowledge of classical history and, more specifically, classical mythology which, whatever other virtues it may have, has always been fruitful ground for poets, playwrights and novelists. (And it still is, as readers of–to name just one modern writer, John Updike– will know).

So, while few schoolchildren today will be expected to read Homer in the original, it is necessary for everyone to have some background knowledge of classical culture. In many American schools, mythology, especially Greek and Roman mythology, is taught as part of the English syllabus, though this is not universally true in, for example, the United Kingdom. There are also many books for a modern audience describing the ancient myths in one aspect or another, including some, of which this is the latest, that aim to provide a simple, background account, without delving deeply into questions of interpretation.

Although this book is chiefly concerned with recounting the myths of classical antiquity in their most commonly accepted form, it is necessary to begin with a few remarks that attempt to provide a rough definition of what a 'myth' is and a brief description of some of the main points of view–old and new, significant and dubious–which have been adopted by those seeking an explanation of the meaning of mythology.

A myth is an imaginative story. The original Greek word for 'myth' meant simply 'words', and carried none of its modern overtone of 'fantasy'. It is clear, on the one hand, that a myth conveys some racial or universal significance, something weightier than the moral contained in a folk story. It is equally clear, on the other hand, that while myths often have some demonstrable link with actual events in a time long ago, they cannot be regarded as 'history', in the sense that Thucydides wrote the history of the Peloponnesian war; not even as 'popular' history embroidered by an imagination unfettered by respect for facts.

It is the nature of man to look for the causes of things around him. Nowadays we expect science to perform this function. But historically, science has seldom provided the right answers—someone once defined scientific progress as the continual correction of previous errors. So science does not present us with ultimate truths; it merely provides explanations that are, on the whole, satisfactory for a particular time. Moreover, most of us really do not understand the explanations of our universe that science provides, we merely accept

The Parthenon, the greatest surviving Doric temple, centre-piece of the Acropolis of Athens, from the north-east. It stands on the site of an earlier temple, which was also dedicated to Athena.

Mount Olympus, the home of the gods, delicately capped by winter's snow. The massif covers a great area and its topmost peak, the highest in Greece, exceeds 300 metres.

Opposite, top:
The Erechtheum, Athens, with the beautiful 'porch of the maidens' at the right and an olive tree in the foreground. Traditionally, the olive tree has always grown on this spot; it was Athena's gift to her city in the contest among the deities for Athens.

Bottom left:
The temple of Olympian Zeus in Athens. The surviving columns—originally there were 104—date from the 2nd century A.D. when the building was completed by the Roman emperor Hadrian, but construction was begun some six and a half centuries earlier.

Bottom right:
The Propylaea, western gateway to the Acropolis. Religious processions passed between the columns up to the sacred precincts.

what the scientists tell us. We accept that the planets exist, or that volcanoes are caused by geological disturbances below the earth's crust, because we are reliably informed that these things are so.

The process of reasoning and experiment that we call science was, of course, non-existent in the time of myth-making people. Those people used the faculty of reason, if at all, in a very limited way, partly because they had little data on which to base a reasoning process.

But besides reason, man has another important faculty not possessed—at least, not demonstrably—by other creatures, the faculty of imagination. To some extent, perhaps, imagination is actually hampered by reason, though most of mankind's most remarkable achievements have involved both. At any rate, man's imaginative faculty was highly developed at a time when his capacity for scientific reasoning barely existed. To put it another way, art is older than science.

The concept of truth is a difficult one, and cannot be entered upon here, but everyone would agree that art conveys a kind of truth no less certainly than science. Thus, a Renaissance painter taking the Fall of Man for his subject, did not think he was providing an accurate, graphic illustration of an actual event. Possibly, he did not even believe that the event actually took place in the way that it was described in his Old Testament source. In painting his picture, he was not concerned with intellectual processes at all. The production of a work of art, which is primarily a work of imagination, comes closer to the way in which a myth originates. It is, however, a different process. Undoubtedly, myths were taken literally in a way that art is not, and to that extent they are allied with science. Science explains a thunderstorm as the result of certain meteorological conditions; myth explains it as the hurling of missiles by a god in the sky. For primitive people, this was a quite sufficient explanation: they had no basis for supposing otherwise. In the same way, a small child will believe that babies are brought by a stork, or found under gooseberry bushes. The capacity to inquire whether the explanation given is correct or not has not been developed.

One hundred years ago, it was widely accepted that myths were a characteristic product of human society in a primitive state, before reason and experiment. It was assumed that all societies passed through a mythic phase in their development. In that phase, man was surrounded by awe-inspiring forces of nature which he could not understand, and he invented stories of supernatural beings to account for them. Eventually, the philosophers came along and made myths redundant, diminishing their status to that of the folk story.

No one today would accept this view of myth-making as an activity restricted to societies in a specific state of development. Every society has its myths, including our own. Myths fill the gap between the questions that mankind asks about the world and the answers he can give, and because new answers tend to raise new questions, that gap will never be closed: a society without myths is unthinkable. All religions are largely based on myth, and it is vital that they should be so. Of course, that does not make them wrong or irrelevant. To draw a clear line between myth and religion would be unwise, as well as virtually impossible, especially in view of the natural tendency for people to regard their own religion as 'truth' and all other religions as 'myth'.

Myths, then, it can reasonably be said, begin as an effort to explain the natural, physical world, and in doing so, they make the world a less frightening place (because its phenomena become more accessible) and offer to man hopes of overcoming, adapting to, or merely

getting along with, nature. The idea of mighty Zeus wrathfully hurling his thunderbolts from Mount Olympus may not be a particularly comfortable notion, but to people in a primitive state of society, it is a great deal less terrifying than the utterly mysterious, inexplicable phenomenon of an electrical storm. In a universe full of strange and momentous events, the myth provides a link between them and humanity, making them familiar, and therefore less frightening. It is the unknown that causes fear; once the flickering shadow is revealed as the effect of moonlight on moving leaves, the nervous child overcomes his terror and no longer sees an evil old woman looming against his bedroom window.

The form that myths take is largely governed by the type of society that creates them. Among settled, farming people there tends to be much emphasis on a mother-earth figure, and developing rituals are often concerned with fertility. Pastoral people, driving their flocks through open country from one grazing place to the next, often in conflict with other groups similarly occupied, frequently have a powerful, protecting figure associated with the sky, which dominates the landscape.

It is important to remember that the Greek myths were very ancient. They originated in some misty past, as alien to 4th-century B.C. Athens as 4th-century Athens is to us. They were, of course, not written down until a comparatively late period.

Myths explain the beginning of the world and are concerned with the activities of gods, or at any rate supernatural beings, who stand for abstract powers and qualities. In the Greek myths, these are the stories of Zeus, his predecessors, his family and other divinities. Another group of myths is concerned with human beings, though they often have close connections with the gods and were sometimes turned into gods themselves. Greek mythology cannot be easily compared with, for example, the Christian religion. Although ancient Jewish myths have some parallels with Greek myths, Greek religion was not based on sacred writings, had no inalienable dogma, and no essential creed. Historically this was a serious weakness, as it rapidly collapsed when confronted by Christianity, but it is also one of its greatest attractions. For Greek religion was, necessarily, very tolerant: there were not, because there could not be, any heretics in ancient Greece – not at any rate, heretics in the sense that the medieval Christian Church gave to the word. It was a practical, convenient kind of religion, which in general (there were some exceptions of course) did not demand too much of the individual while remaining closely attached to ordinary, everyday life. It had some monsters, but on

The stadium at Olympia. The vaulted arch, practically unknown in classical Greece, dates from the 2nd century B.C. and is one of the earliest examples.

The view from the Parthenon, on the Acropolis, north-east to Mount Lycabettus. According to tradition, the early settlers of Athens intended to build their citadel on Mount Lycabettus (rather than the Acropolis) but were forced to reject the site because it had no water.

Part of the palace of Knossos, Crete, looking west across the central court towards the throne room.

The store rooms of the palace of Knossos. These huge jars—*pithoi*—contained grain, olives and oil.

The famous lions in the precinct of Apollo at Delos, made of marble from Naxos (at one time the protector of Delos). Five of the original nine survive very nearly intact, and there is another at Venice.

the whole very little magic; much violence and cruelty, but very little evil. Its gods were, as personalities, thoroughly human. It had no mystical prophets claiming to represent the word of God, but was known through the works of poets, who had no claim to be theological experts of any kind, merely good poets. The persecution and punishment of people on grounds of religion, so familiar a theme of Western history in post-classical times, was wholly alien to the Greeks. They would have found it hard to understand such an institution as the Inquisition; Calvin would have puzzled them no less. The content of Greek religion varied considerably, not only in time but also from place to place, but the Greeks found nothing particularly strange in that, certainly nothing to make them throw up their beliefs in despair.

The question of the significance of myths is endlessly fascinating and has given rise to many very diverse speculations by scholars of different disciplines. By its very nature, mythology encourages exotic etiological theories. Some myths can be profitably interpreted as allegories, stories of a more or less homely sort constructed to embody profound truths about the nature of existence which simple people could not be expected to apprehend. While this view can often lead to revealing interpretations, it has one serious drawback. Someone must have constructed the allegory, but to have done so would have required far greater knowledge of science and morals than was available at the time, far greater than ordinary people possessed. The apparent allegorical significance of the Greek myths is often the product of later reasoning.

The same objection applies to the interpretation of Greek myths as symbolic presentations of religious beliefs. This too has been the cause of much highly ingenious and superficially compelling detective work; but it presupposes that an elaborate religion existed *before* the myths were invented, a very improbable supposition for which there is hardly a shred of serious evidence. Myths do not originate in this way, and although in certain senses myths often are symbolic, to treat them as a kind of camouflage or cryptogram, to be solved like a crossword puzzle, is generally misleading. People are fond of mysteries of this sort, witness the kind of popularity enjoyed today by books which suggest that there is a section of the western Atlantic (the so-called Bermuda Triangle) which is deadly to ships, or those which, on the basis of 'evidence' that no serious scholar could possibly accept, maintain that in the past the Earth was visited by creatures from outer space. It is all too easy to find subtle enigmas in Greek mythology where none exist.

The trouble with most theories about the significance of classical mythology is that they fail to take into account the state of knowledge and state of mind of the myth-making people. It is difficult for, say, a German to think like a Chinese, and it is still more difficult for post-industrial man to put himself in the place of an ancient Greek (especially a pre-classical one). The fact that, in some ways, the Greeks seem closer, or more sympathetic, to us than many later societies only aggravates the problem; for when we are struck by the pertinence of Plato's philosophy or the humour of Aristophanes' comedy, we tend too easily to think 'How modern!' or 'How like us!' It is difficult to remember that tales, far older than Plato or Aristophanes, which seem pure fantasy to us would not have seemed so to people who knew nothing of the world beyond their own small country. We know the sky is not made of bronze because scientists have told us what it *is* made of. If we had to depend on our own untutored imagination, a great bronze dome would not seem so absurd an explanation.

The temple of Apollo at Corinth, with its massive Doric columns which are fashioned from single blocks of stone, not built up from thick discs—as in the next colour plate.

The Greeks themselves were frequently guilty of explaining their myths in falsely rational terms. A contemporary of Aristotle explained those curious creatures, the Centaurs, as evolving from a band of mounted hunters in Thessaly who were employed to rid the country of wild bulls. While the story cannot be completely discounted, there is no reason for believing it and, though appealing in its sheer ingenuity, it arises chiefly from the writer's failure to realize that his ancestors would not have considered the existence of creatures half horse and half man as improbable as he did. There is no cause to adopt a prosaic origin of such legends. People were quite capable of conceiving of Centaurs without the assistance of bull-hunting cavalry.

Another theory about the Greek gods popular in ancient times was that they were originally human–kings and generals engaged in dynastic politics and war. Some of the legends are extremely difficult to fit into this theory, however they are explained in realistic terms. But as some men certainly were turned into gods in Greek mythology, the theory at first seems quite promising. One obvious difficulty is that, in order to turn men into gods, it was first necessary to have an idea of what gods were: in order to make a purse out of a sow's ear you must have a good idea of what a purse *is*.

Although it is often difficult in Greek mythology to divide gods from heroes, it seems certain that Zeus was always a god, never a king of Crete. But if the gods were not persons, can they have been personifications–that is, humanized representations of natural phenomena, or abstract qualities? Here again, there are some obvious connections, as the various deities are frequently associated with a particular quality, or virtue. But this interpretation runs into the objections made against others–that it assumes the existence of systems of thought too advanced for the myth-making people. Other mythologies tend to suggest that there is usually a distinct difference between a deity and his or her particular element or quality. Poseidon was not the sea, he was the god of the sea, who lived in it and controlled it. Our knowledge of other mythologies also suggests that the sources of myths are more various than this limited explanation would allow.

The remains of the citadel of Tiryns, the alleged birthplace of Heracles. This Mycenaean city was excavated by Schliemann in 1884–86, his last great discovery in Greece.

The temple of Poseidon at Cape Sounion, overlooking the sea, and a welcome landfall for Athenian sailors making for the Piraeus (the port of Athens). Menelaus of Sparta was delayed here when Apollo struck down his pilot.

The Greeks, enterprising and adventurous sailors, colonized much of southern Italy and the island of Sicily. They took their beliefs, and their unmistakable building style, with them and this temple to the sailors' god can still be seen at Paestum, south of Salerno.

In fact, few modern scholars find it possible to accept any all-embracing explanation of the myths of the Greeks, or the myths of any other people. In the first place, the early Greeks were not a single people, they were Dorians, Ionians, and so on, and some Greek myths were drawn from other – that is non-Greek – sources. However, the myths did not all spring into existence at one time. Some are very old, others more recent. Some may have descended through the centuries in more or less their original form, while others have been elaborated, altered and reinvented by later writers. It can be shown that the earliest surviving accounts of many myths were themselves reworkings of earlier accounts, now lost.

What makes myths important, and distinguishes them from legends, is that they clearly have some kind of universal significance for humanity. The many close parallels that exist between the myths of entirely different cultures, though it is easy to make too much of these similarities, show that mythology must fulfil some fundamental purpose. Psychologists have, not surprisingly, found mythology a rewarding area of work. Of the great pioneers in psychology, Jung seems nearest in sympathy to mythology, with his important theory of the collective unconscious. But Freud and his followers are more closely associated with the Greek myths. Who has not heard of the Oedipus complex?

A beehive-shaped ceiling at Mycenae, made from expertly cut stones without the use of mortar, about 1300–1500 B.C. Schliemann believed these extraordinary structures to be treasuries – very reasonably as he found treasure within them – but they were more likely tombs, the treasures of a great man having been buried with him.

However, while psychologists may find useful and meaningful illustrations of their doctrines in mythology, it is rather doubtful whether psychology, though it may offer any number of interesting insights, can explain the birth of a myth. Freud's theory about the rivalry between son and father for the affections of the mother may be accurate, and the Oedipus story a beautiful illustration of it, but it is hard to believe that the psychological theory explains the origin of the story, or that the story evolved as a – conscious or unconscious – parable of it.

If classical mythology has been useful to modern psychology (rather more than the other way around), it has been much less useful to modern anthropology. This is not really surprising when the mythological world is compared with the world of primitive man as we know it from other sources. Perhaps the chief attraction of the world of the Greek myths, superficially at any rate, is that it is on the whole a cheerful and attractive place. It is largely covered by woods (not much trace of them now, incidentally, though for that the depradations of the ubiquitous goat may be largely to blame), indeed of 'sylvan glades', as poets used to say, rather than thorny undergrowth. They are inhabited by charming female creatures, very quick on their feet in order to escape the intentions of lecherous, but not particularly threatening, masculine creatures. There is a good deal of eating and drinking, many pranks, often admittedly rather crude, and much laughter. Of course the myths are also full of violence and murder, and the story of the House of Atreus as related by Aeschylus, for example, is not exactly light entertainment; but the overall impression is one of good cheer.

Nothing, of course, could be less like primitive man's experience of the world he lived in. He did not frolic in sun-dappled glades, nor spy on nymphs frolicking by a stream. He slunk fearfully along dark forest paths, and cringed from ominous noises in the undergrowth. As an illustration of the existence of the people of the time, myths need careful interpretation and usually remain of very limited usefulness.

Nevertheless, all interpretations of the myths have something to offer, whether allegorical or symbolical, psychological or anthropological. But what of myth as history?

In a sense, myths were the ancient history of the Greeks. Handbooks of mythology are not a recent development: the Greeks had their own handbooks and guides to the complicated relationships of the gods. It is true that they also invented new myths, but they did not do so in the sense that a modern writer invents a short story. New myths generally followed long-established conventions, and their originators probably felt they were merely elucidating the truth.

There are certain fairly common themes in the Greek myths, such as the overthrow of kings by their sons-in-law or their grandsons, which may probably reflect a time in which a young man gained power by marrying the king's daughter and overthrowing the king. If so, it was a time before the arrival of the Dorians and probably as far back as 2000 B.C., in the early Mycenean period, if not even earlier.

The best-known example of a myth with strong historical connections – more accurately described as legend – is the story of the Trojan War, the subject of Homer's *Iliad*. Although the story was generally discounted in later antiquity, when no trace of Troy remained, during the Middle Ages it was widely believed in Western Europe. Indeed, there was a common literary convention that the European races were descended from the Trojan heroes, who scattered after the fall of Troy. Later, the historical basis was completely discounted, and the general opinion became that Homer's story was just that—a story, with no foundation in fact: Troy never existed. Then, in the 19th century, Heinrich Schliemann, an inspired amateur archaeologist, actually discovered Troy, on the hill of Hissarlik, close to the Dardanelles. (Later research discovered the remains of nine or ten cities on the site, of which Homer's Troy was the sixth or seventh.) So there *was* a Troy after all, and there was a Trojan war, at about the time described by Homer (around 1180 B.C.). The probability is, however, that Homer's account is a long way from the actual events. The war was probably fought over trade and shipping, and grew out of Greek attempts to break Troy's control of the Dardanelles. The abduction of Helen, if it occurred, is unlikely to have been the chief cause of such prolonged hostilities. Other examples of the myth-makers' embroidery, whether by Homer or some predecessor (or successor), are more obvious: we find it hard to believe, for instance, that Achilles was invulnerable to wounds anywhere except in his heel, still less the explanation for his impenetrability, and the interventions of the gods are, obviously, mythical. More recently, sad to say, scholars have come to doubt the authenticity of the Trojan horse—the hollow, wooden structure, presented as a gift, in which the Greeks smuggled men into the city.

Legend, which supposes a historical basis, is often inextricably mingled with myth in Greek mythology. Thus, if the story of the Trojan war is a legend, the explanation of the invulnerability of Achilles is a myth. Moreover, as time goes on, some of the myths turn into a form that is neither myth nor legend but merely story-telling, where the only purpose is amusement: the story of Pygmalion and Galatea, for example, is pure romance. Here, credibility is not

A view of the great sacred precincts of Delos, birthplace of Apollo and an important centre of his cult.

Opposite:
The purpose of the Tholos, most familiar of the surviving buildings at Delphi (the columns were re-erected in modern times), remains unknown. It stands in the sanctuary of Athena. Dionysus was also represented at Delphi, though the chief subject of veneration here was the oracle of Apollo, whose influence spread far beyond Greece.

Above:
The ruins of Troy VI. The excavation of the site by Heinrich Schliemann in the 19th century proved that Homer's city really existed, although, except for the archaeologist, the ruins of Troy offer no spectacular revelations to the modern visitor nourished on Homer.

Centre:
The stadium of Delphi, the highest point in the sacred precinct of Apollo, the home of the supreme oracle of classic times.

Bottom:
Eleusis, the chief centre of the cult of Demeter. The Eleusinian mysteries were the most closely guarded secret of antiquity. No initiate—not even emperors—ever betrayed them.

19

The great theatre of Epidauros, during restoration. Since this photograph was taken, restoration has been completed, and a festival of Greek tragedy is held there every year.

required. However, credibility is not an intrinsic quality: one man's myth is another man's fairy story.

Practically all Greek literature is concerned with mythology, and our mythological sources include virtually everything of Greek poetry that has survived, plus some works that we know of at second or third hand. If there is such a thing as 'pure' myth we do not have any, for the earliest works we have are the *Iliad* and the *Odyssey* of Homer. (The dispute over whether Homer was one or several people will probably never be settled: it seems possible that the *Iliad* is, in the main, by a single hand, but the *Odyssey* may have been written later, and by more than one author). Homer collected traditional stories in about the 9th century B.C., for a contemporary audience, and he adapted his material accordingly. (Of course, Homer did not actually 'write' anything; but his words were probably written down quite soon afterwards.)

Next in importance after Homer is Hesiod, in particular his *Theogony* (again, there is some doubt over his actual authorship), a long, mythological poem from about the 8th century B.C., which is the earliest account of the beginning of the world and the gods.

The lyric poet, Pindar, writing about 500 B.C., frequently repeated or alluded to myths in his odes to the victors at the Olympic Games and other, similar festivals; he often invented or adjusted myths to suit his immediate purpose. Still more important are the great tragedians of the 5th century, Aeschylus, Sophocles and Euripides, whose plots derive from the same sources as Pindar's poems. Like Pindar – and, indeed, most other writers – they made alterations where they considered them necessary, but with one exception all their plays are on mythological subjects. A playwright of a different sort, Aristophanes, also frequently referred to myths, as did philosophers like Plato and historians like Herodotus. Several later writers produced what might be called popular guides to mythology in one form or another, one of the most important being Apollodorus, who wrote the only complete account to survive the centuries in the 1st or 2nd century A.D.

There is also much material to be found in Latin writers, especially in Ovid. By that time, however, the Greek myths belonged to a very distant past. Ovid, in fact, found the ancient myths more remote than we do, and cheerfully advised his readers that he intended to 'prate of ancient poets' monstrous lies'. Although more of the myths appear in Ovid than in any other author, he used them merely as the raw material for his excellent and entertaining verse; as a guide to Greek mythology, Ovid is unreliable.

The view across the Agora at Athens, looking east towards the restored portico of Attalus II, king of Pergamon (2nd century B.C.), reconstructed through American munificence and scholarship. The Acropolis is on the right.

The fortress-rock of Corinth. This city so famous in myth and history was totally destroyed by the Romans in 196 B.C., and the ruins now evident are those of the reconstruction carried out by Julius Caesar.

21

Crete

A Cycladic fertility figure or goddess, in marble, now in the British Museum.

The name 'Greeks' does not appear in Homer, where the Greek heroes are usually called Achaeans. Though the Greeks came to think of themselves as a nation, of a sort, that was a late development, and they, like most other races, were a mixture of peoples.

The pre-Greek inhabitants of what is now mainland Greece, about five thousand years ago, were a scattered farming people, of whom little is known. They were rapidly absorbed by the successive waves of invaders, called Aeolians and Ionians, which began about that time. The first arrivals came in fairly small numbers, and probably settled down quite peaceably, apparently giving up a nomadic way of life for a more settled existence as farmers. They settled mainly in the east and in Crete and Cyprus, for they were also a sea-going people. Their tools were made of stone, and they probably spoke an early Indo-European language. Their gods may have been the Aryan trinity of sky-gods, Indra, Varuna and Mitra, while the original inhabitants, like other prehistoric communities in the eastern Mediterranean area, would most likely have worshipped a mother goddess. Women were regarded as, if not the more powerful, the more important and mysterious sex because they produced offspring, and so kept the race going; it was probably not realized that men made any contribution to this vital process. The problems of ecumenicalism being then non-existent, the native religion of the mother goddess would have merged quite comfortably with the new, Aryan deities, who were perhaps regarded as her children.

During the early Bronze Age, which began in Greece about 2500 B.C., life must have been fairly peaceful in spite of the arrival of newcomers, as villages were built without defence-works. The new settlers, while preferring the warmer and drier eastern parts of Greece, gradually spread into the west as well. They made beautiful pottery and, in the islands, lead models of their all-important ships. They were 'people of the sea', in the Egyptian description, and had control of the carrying trade in the eastern Mediterranean. Their religion revolved around a female deity, and they left many small figures of her in stone.

From about 1900 B.C., life in mainland Greece became less peaceful, as a rougher and more numerous lot of newcomers forced their way in, possibly from the west. Though these people were more primitive in many ways, they introduced the horse and the potter's wheel and, in the guarded opinion of many experts, they were the first people to speak Greek. These 'delighters in horses' (Hesiod's epithet) were the founders of the Greek race.

Hesiod divided the successive waves of invaders of prehistoric Greece into three groups, the Ionians, the Aeolians and the Dorians, who are believed to have arrived about 1000 B.C. Homer's Achaean's were predecessors of the Dorians.

Integration did not occur so easily with these later invaders. In classical Sparta the Helots, descendants of earlier inhabitants, were the slaves of their Dorian masters. However, the pre-Dorian Mycenaean civilization (so-called after the discoveries made by Schliemann at Mycenae), which is basically the civilization of the myths, was the result of a fusion of cultures.

As we now know, the first Greek civilization, pre-dating Mycenae, was in existence and undergoing more or less continual development from the end of the New Stone Age. Its centre was not on the Greek mainland at all, but at Knossos and other places in the island of Crete, the birthplace, according to one version of the myth, of Zeus himself.

The Greek religion, although it has been shown to reflect influences from many other places, including Egypt and the Middle East, had its true origin in Bronze-Age Crete. Yet the very existence of Minoan civilization, as it is called after the legendary King Minos, was unknown until Sir Arthur Evans and other archaeologists undertook their excavations in Crete at the beginning of this century. They discovered what was first thought to be a Mycenaean civilization (Mycenae itself had only recently been discovered), but turned out to be older. The revelations of the palace of Knossos, with its vivid frescoes of aristocratic young men and women, its astonishingly efficient systems of plumbing and lighting, its strange underground chambers, its curious 'snake-goddesses' and, above all, its sinister sport of 'bull-dancing'—Knossos was a sensational discovery, perhaps even more remarkable than Schliemann's discovery of Troy.

The people of Crete, like the Stone-Age settlers in mainland Greece, probably came from the Middle East. It is certain that, at a very early period, Crete was in contact with Egypt, and the examples of cultural similarities between the two countries are numerous. For example, the symbol of a Nilotic goddess in the 4th millennium B.C. was a double shield of the type found by Sir Arthur Evans in the palace of King Minos at Knossos. Styles of dress in Crete were practically identical with styles in Libya, west of the Nile delta, and it may be that people from this region came to Crete as refugees after Lower Egypt was conquered, about 3000 B.C. Certainly there was close and continual contact. Some beans discovered by Evans in stone jars at Knossos were recognized by his Cretan workmen as identical with beans still being imported to Crete from Egypt five thousand years later.

A Cycladic head dating from the 3rd millennium B.C. The Cyclades are the islands 'circling' Delos. This remarkable sculpture, which might equally belong to the early 20th century A.D., probably represents a god. Traditionally, the inhabitants of the Cyclades originated in Asia Minor and were driven from the islands by King Minos.

An overall view of the central part of the palace of King Minos. A notable feature of this great structural complex is the absence of fortifications—very different from Mycenaean sites—which is evidence of the maritime supremacy of the Minoans.

Above:
The palace at Knossos, showing the south Propylon, with columns restored by Sir Arthur Evans, and the 'horns of consecration'.

Opposite:
The 'Bull Portico' at Knossos. The red columns were originally wood, but Evans had to use concrete in their reconstruction.

Crete developed steadily during the third millennium B.C.: population increased, towns were built, trade contacts maintained. More dramatic developments took place soon after 2000 B.C. (the Middle Minoan period). The use of metals, chiefly bronze, made stone-cutting possible, and the great palaces were built. Knossos was the largest; although it probably did not possess complete political control at this time, it represented a culture which, with slight local variations, spanned the island. The potter's wheel came into use, the brilliant frescoes appeared, and the arts reached a high point. The people, or at least those who lived in the palaces, were rich; and their riches came from trade. Their command of the sea was unchallenged, and they possessed commercial colonies throughout the Aegean Sea. There is little solid evidence of this Minoan maritime empire, barring tradition; but the tradition was strong in classical Greece and was accepted, for instance, by that judicious historian, Thucydides. Painting on pottery reveals the Cretans' interest in marine subjects.

Right:
The steps of the 'theatre', or dancing floor, where cult rituals took place at Knossos. The precise composition and meaning of these performances may remain a mystery for ever.

Below:
The royal way from the dancing floor leads out of the palace towards the site of the city, where excavation still goes on. This is believed to be the oldest paved road in Europe.

An early Minoan seal showing, apparently, a female goddess with a priestess in attendance. The offerings of fruits suggest a fertility rite. These seals are not uncommon. It was his curiosity about such objects that set Sir Arthur Evans on the road that led to his discoveries at Knossos.

By about 1600 B.C., Crete was a great power. Roads, guarded by forts, spanned the island, and Knossos was the seat of an efficient and complex government: its size and complexity were truly labyrinthine. The population of the island probably exceeded a million. The form of writing known as Linear B script, now known to be an early form of Greek, became universal. The king at Knossos rightly regarded himself as the head of a great empire, equal to the Egyptian or the Hittite empire.

The eminence of Minoan Crete ended about 1400 B.C. It is not clear what was responsible, whether invasion from the mainland or some natural disaster. If the latter, it was followed by occupation by Greeks, or Myceneans, from the mainland. About 1000 B.C. the Dorians appeared and the last physical remnants of Minoan civilization disappeared, to survive, however, in myth and legend.

Religion in Crete no doubt began, as in other places, with a superstitious reverence for natural phenomena and with cults associated with Man's most urgent needs. Stylized versions of objects important to him were venerated, along with creatures representing especially desirable qualities. Thus the bull is a symbol of manly strength, and the snake a symbol of fertility, in many places besides Crete.

Equally, it is not surprising that the Minoans had a mother goddess as the centre of their religion. Evans discovered on the engraved stone seals of the Early Minoan Period numerous representations of a female figure who is clearly the object of veneration. Sometimes she is shown with a male figure, who is usually smaller and obviously inferior. In the Middle Period, statuettes were made showing the mother-goddess in the dress of an aristocratic lady of the court—wasp-waisted and bare-breasted, with an ornate headdress. Evans identified her with Rhea, mother of Zeus, but she probably had a number of different aspects, of which Rhea was one. The female statuettes, which may sometimes represent the attendants of the goddess, are often shown with a snake wound around the arms. Snakes are fairly common in fertility cults, though Evans suggested that the

The throne room of King Minos.

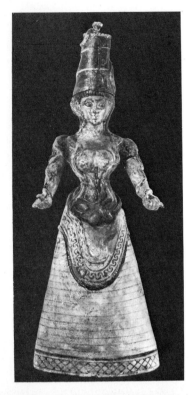

These small figures from Knossos are one of the most famous of archaeological finds. They may represent a mother goddess or, perhaps more likely, a priestess. Snakes are prominent as fertility symbols in many cultures. The figures are dressed in the normal fashion of the Minoan court.

figure with a snake represented the goddess in her aspect as 'Lady of the Underworld'. This idea, which would not meet wide acceptance now, largely resulted from Evans's brilliantly imaginative ideas about the Cretan attitude to the Earth.

In the palace at Knossos, Evans discovered a number of sunken chambers, with steps leading down, at first assumed to be baths. He called them 'lustral areas', believing that some kind of anointing rite had taken place there. More of these areas were discovered in the palace at Phaestos and at other sites. Evans was convinced that they had a religious significance, and were linked with Earth worship.

There was another type of chamber in the Minoan palaces which seemed more definitely connected with Earth worship. These were deep, underground chambers with a massive, central, stone pillar, which Evans called 'pillar crypts'. A drain near the pillar suggested that some type of sacrifice had taken place in them, and the pillars sometimes bore the common Cretan symbol of the double-headed axe.

The excavations at Knossos showed that it had been occupied for well over 2,000 years – throughout the Aegean Bronze Age – with more or less continual development. Yet there were clear signs of major catastrophes occurring at several widely separated times during that period. On the basis of other evidence, Evans connected these catastrophes with major earthquakes.

The discovery of the skulls of two large oxen, clearly a sacrificial offering, in the basement of a house which had almost certainly been destroyed by earthquake, was the final piece of evidence suggesting that the Cretans had sacrificed bulls to an Earth god in an attempt to prevent him shaking the earth; possibly the lustral areas, sunk deep into the ground, once witnessed some rite of propitiation to the Earth-Shaker. Greek mythology provided corroborating evidence. Did not Homer, in the *Iliad*, remark on the delight of the Earth-Shaker in bulls? Did not Minos enrage Poseidon by substituting an inferior animal for the splendid bull he had promised to sacrifice?

Nevertheless, very little is known for certain about the actual religious practices of the Minoans, and their mythology can only be guessed at by what descended to their successors. In particular, the acrobatic bull-vaulting so brilliantly displayed in the famous fresco at Knossos remains a mystery. It is usually described as a 'sport', but it must have been a grim kind of sport. Experienced rodeo riders are adamant that it is impossible to perform the feat apparently depicted, in which a young man or girl seizes the horns of the bull as it charges towards him and, being swung up into the air as the bull

A funeral procession, found on a sarcophagus at Hagia Triada in the south of Crete. Bulls were offered as sacrifices in the funeral rites.

Opposite, top:
The bull-leaping rite, a figure now in the British Museum. No one really knows exactly what it was. Experienced American rodeo performers have insisted that such acrobatics are scarcely possible without the likelihood of mortal injury.

Left:
One of the famous Cretan gold cups of about 1500 B.C. showing the capture of a wild bull by means of a decoy cow—tactics recalling the myth of Pasiphae. The cups were found at Vaphio in the Peloponnese and are now in the National Museum at Athens.

One of the lesser-known palace sites in Crete is at Mallia, on the north coast east of Knossos. Rich finds continue and testify to the splendour of Minoan culture.

jerks its head up, somersaults on to the bull's back and leaps off. It seems unlikely that the performers would have survived, and it may not be too fanciful to suppose that here is the origin of the seven young men and seven virgins annually sacrificed to the Minotaur by King Minos, the legendary king after whom the Bronze Age civilization in Crete is named.

Minos may have been an actual king of Crete: Homer says he ruled for eight years. Or, perhaps more likely, the name may have been a title, like Pharaoh. However, in Greek mythology, Minos was a very definite individual.

Though a mortal, he was a son of Zeus. His mother was Europa, whom Zeus had seduced in the guise of—a bull! The seduction is usually described as a rape, but there is a strong suggestion that Europa suspected the beautiful, tame, white bull was something other than it seemed. At any rate, Europa climbed upon the bull's back, whereupon he carried her rapidly off to Crete. There she in due course gave birth to Minos, as well as one or two other sons.

As king of Crete, Minos made the bad mistake of offending Poseidon over the matter of the sacrifice of a bull, mentioned above, and the god of the sea took an unkind revenge by afflicting Minos's wife, Pasiphae, with an outrageous sexual appetite. Finding men unsatisfying, she lusted only for the bull that Minos had neglected to sacrifice. The bull, a more normal creature, was naturally uninterested, but Pasiphae eventually achieved her desire by concealing herself in a dummy cow. This deception was arranged by the remarkable Athenian engineer then resident at Knossos, Daedalus, who fashioned a hollow cow out of wood; but it resulted in the eventual birth of a horrible monster, the Minotaur, half man and half bull and wholly carnivorous. (There are examples of man-bull creatures in Minoan art.) To restrain this monster, Daedalus constructed a complicated Labyrinth in which it was confined. (It is not hard to imagine that the vast palace of Knossos, with its numerous chambers and passages, appeared like a labyrinth to the Mycenaean Greeks who arrived about 1400 B.C.).

At about this time, Athens became subject to Knossos, after Minos had sent an expedition to conquer it. The Cretan attack had been provoked by the death of Minos's son while a visitor in Athens, and once more a bull was involved in the incident. The king of Athens had rather thoughtlessly sent the youth to capture a wild bull, and he was killed. (Methods of capturing wild bulls are shown in relief on Minoan gold cups: one method was to entangle it in a net; another, more interesting, involved a decoy cow, which dallied with the bull while the hunter slipped a noose on its hind leg; perhaps there is some dim connection with Pasiphae's means of seduction).

As overlord of Athens, Minos demanded a stiff tribute—fourteen Athenian lads and lasses annually to feed to the Minotaur. After some years, Theseus arrived in Athens and volunteered to be a member of the unlucky party. One of the greatest of the heroes of Greek mythology, Theseus was, one might say, in mid-career at this point. The rest of his story will appear later.

When Theseus arrived in Crete, Minos's daughter, Ariadne, promptly fell in love with him, and asked Daedalus to show her a way to get Theseus out of the Labyrinth. Daedalus advised tying a long string to the entrance and spinning it out behind. Theseus followed this advice, discovered the Minotaur in the depths of the Labyrinth, and killed him. Picking up the string, he followed it easily back to the entrance. As night fell, he made his escape from Crete with Ariadne (and, presumably, the grateful young Athenians).

The excavated palace at Phaistos, second only to Knossos among Minoan sites and investigated by Italian archaeologists at the same time as Evans was working at Knossos.

So far so good; but at Naxos things began to go wrong. Theseus deserted Ariadne there, for one of several possible reasons: because he was tired of her; because he had lost his memory due to a spell; because Dionysus carried her off. At any rate, Dionysus took her away to Lemnos, where she had several children by him. That Theseus had lost his memory seems the preferable explanation, for he also forgot to raise white sails on his ship when he came in sight of Athens. This was to have been a signal to his father that he was still alive. Seeing the black sails, the anguished parent assumed the worst and, in his grief, threw himself from the Acropolis and was killed.

Meanwhile, King Minos seems to have been uncharacteristically passive. But now he stirred himself to action. He was not unnaturally angry with Daedalus, who had made Theseus's exploits possible, and imprisoned him, with his son Icarus, in the now-vacant Labyrinth, presumably posting a strong guard at the entrance. Daedalus' ingenuity was again equal to the occasion, and he equipped himself and Icarus with wings. As they soared away over the Aegean, Icarus, carried away with the wonderful sensation, disregarded his father's flight instructions, which included a warning not to fly near the sun in case it melted the glue on the wings. The glue did melt, and Icarus plunged to his death in the sea.

Above :
A Roman relief showing Daedalus putting the finishing touches to the dummy cow he constructed for Pasiphae, who is inspecting the work.

Right :
Daedalus at work on the wings with which he and his son Icarus escaped from captivity in Crete. A Roman relief.

Daedalus flew on alone, and eventually settled at the court of King Cocalus, in Sicily. But Minos was determined to find him, though he had to scour the world. He set out, taking with him a spiral shell and announcing to everyone he met that he would give a rich reward to the man who could pass a thread through the shell. He knew that Daedalus would be well disguised, but he knew also that Daedalus would be unable to resist such a challenge to his technical ingenuity.

At length Minos arrived in Sicily. King Cocalus said he would pass the thread through the shell, and handed the problem to Daedalus, who provided a solution as apt as the method of extracting Theseus from the Labyrinth. He tied one end of the thread to an ant, bored a hole in the shell, and waited for the ant to find its way out. Seeing the shell threaded, Minos realized that the wanted man was at hand, and demanded that Cocalus should surrender him. Cocalus agreed, but first arranged an entertainment for Minos. But 'after his bath Minos was undone by the daughters of Cocalus'. The implication seems to be that Minos was the victim of a plot, perhaps arranged by Cocalus because he did not want to surrender Daedalus, who is said to have undertaken many projects for the king. It is very mysterious. However, it seems to have been the end of Minos, who next appears as a judge of the dead in the Underworld.

A powerfully erotic relief of Ariadne and Dionysus, who found the abandoned maiden at Naxos after Theseus had left her there.

Zeus and Man

The decline of the Earth-goddess and the rise of the Sky-god Zeus can be taken as representative of the fall of Minoan civilization and the rise of the more warlike, more mobile Mycenaeans. Of course, one culture was not simply replaced by another: nothing could be plainer than the influence of the Minoans on the Mycenaeans, and the initial difficulties of Zeus may suggest the conflict and adjustment of a new order with the old.

The gods of the Greeks were more human than most; apart from their supernatural powers, they behaved like ordinary men and women and were regarded so, without disrespect, by the poets. The gods were not, for example, regarded as creators of the world.

In the beginning, says Hesiod, there was Chaos, which means not what it has come to mean since but merely a yawning void. Next came Earth, Gaea (perhaps to be identified with the Minoan Earth-goddess). It is not clear if or how Earth emerged from Chaos. Another tradition has Oceanus – Water – in place of Chaos. In Hesiod, Oceanus is the offspring of Earth, though he surrounded her on all sides (medieval world maps show the earth surrounded by water). From Chaos also appeared Eros, the generative force, or Love, as well as Erebus (Darkness) and Night, who together produced Air and Day. (Another version says that Eros sprang from an egg laid by Night – a particularly attractive idea).

So far, we are dealing with philosophical concepts rather than thoroughly anthropomorphic conceptions, but in the next generation true personalities appear. Gaea (Earth), single-handed as it were, gave birth to Uranus (Heaven), and together they produced a string of children who included Cronos (the Roman Saturn), the youngest, the 'twisted thinker' and 'most dread of children', who hated his father. The children of Gaea and Uranus were called the Titans; on the whole they are dim and misty figures, representing forces of nature, and though several of them appear in important myths, they are probably not – or not all – Greek in origin. Besides the Titans, Gaea and Uranus also produced a rather weird collection of giants and monsters, such as the Cyclops, some of whom will also reappear later. Meanwhile, the line that leads to Zeus must be followed.

Uranus was jealous of his children and used to hide them inside Earth, which displeased Gaea. She took advantage of her youngest son's hostility to his father and persuaded him to castrate Uranus, a grisly deed which he accomplished with a saw-toothed sickle. Cronos hurled the severed parts away from him, but drops of blood fell upon Earth, who conceived again and brought forth the Furies and the Giants. The testicles of Uranus fell into the sea; foam was thrown up, and from the foam emerged Aphrodite.

The appearance of the goddess of love, the first thoroughly womanly creature, who 'strikes fond love into the hearts of all', comes, one may think, opportunely in this tale of horrid deeds and monsters. Aphrodite was also, in origin, probably a non-Greek goddess, though possibly a mother goddess from Cyprus. In Homer, she is the daughter of Zeus.

The family violence was far from over. The story of Cronos and his children oddly echoes the story of Uranus. For Cronos too feared his offspring, having learned from Gaea and Uranus that one of them would overthrow him. To prevent this, he swallowed each one as soon as his consort, Rhea, also a child of Uranus and Gaea, and incidentally bearing a name shared by the Minoan mother goddess, produced it. (To point out the frequent significance of Freudian psychology in Greek mythology would grow tiresome). When her youngest son, Zeus, was born, Rhea hid him away in a Cretan cave and gave Cronos a stone to swallow instead.

When Zeus grew up, the battle with Cronos began. Zeus had many allies, for Rhea had persuaded Cronos to cough up some at least of his swallowed offspring, and Zeus had released from Tartaros (a deep place in the earth) the offspring of Uranus. In gratitude they gave him power over thunder and lightning. Zeus, whose headquarters were established on Mount Olympus, was also supported by Styx, the fearsome underworld river spirit, and her children, while Cronos was supported by his fellow-Titans with one or two exceptions, such as Prometheus.

Gaea, or Earth, surrounded by her fruits. A mosaic of the Roman period from Aleppo. Originally, no doubt, Gaea was a local goddess, identified with a specific locality rather than the whole earth.

35

Crete: the view across the remains of the Minoan palace of Hagia Triada to the distant Mount Ida. The infant Zeus was hidden in a cave in the mountains of Crete to save him from his father, Cronus.

Opposite:
A bronze head of Nike (Victory), in Homer an abstraction merely, but at one time linked with Athena. There is a delightful little temple to Nike on the Acropolis. In Rome she was assimilated to the goddess Victoria and was, not surprisingly given the Romans' priorities, a more important deity than she ever was in Greece.

It seems reasonable to suppose that the long battle between Zeus and the Titans may represent conflict between the pre-Hellenic inhabitants of Greece and invading newcomers. Zeus, like the invaders, was eventually victorious. The Titans were imprisoned in Tartaros, except for Atlas, whose great strength was mobilised to hold sky and earth apart. In some stories, the Titans reappear later, so Zeus presumably released them when his power was secure. Of the fate of Cronos himself there are several versions. Plutarch, writing about A.D. 100, had him permanently sleeping on a holy island near Britain. In some works he is the king of Elysium (paradise). A Latin legend makes him the founder of a city on the future site of Rome.

The defeat of the Titans did not make the rule of Zeus perfectly secure. He had to face a number of challenges to his power, including a rebellion of the serpent-footed Giants, who were born to Gaea from the blood of Uranus when Cronos castrated him. After another terrific battle, in which the Giants used whole oak trees as missiles, they were defeated by Zeus, who was assisted not only by his fellow deities but also by his son Heracles. The defeated Giants were locked away under various volcanic islands.

But Gaea produced yet another monstrous child, more formidable than (though similar to) the Giants. This was Typhon, a winged serpent-man, whose mere appearance so terrified the other Olympians that they turned themselves into animals and fled. Zeus himself was temporarily defeated, for Typhon gained possession of his sword (a weapon similar to that used by Cronos against Uranus) and cut out the sinews of Zeus' hands and feet, leaving him helpless in a cave. But Hermes and Pan got the sinews back and Zeus was restored. Taking up his thunderbolts, he renewed his battle against Typhon and, after a running fight around the known world, defeated him and imprisoned him under Mount Etna, where his roars and belches may still be heard.

This made Zeus' position secure, for the other Olympians accepted him as supreme and he reached agreement with his brothers, the other two sons of Cronos, by a division of the inheritance which gave Zeus the sky, Poseidon the sea and Hades the underworld.

Rhea offers Cronus a stone disguised as their latest infant. An Athenian vase of the 5th century B.C., now in the Metropolitan Museum, New York.

The battle between Zeus, brandishing his thunderbolt, and the winged, serpentine giant, Typhon. A red-figure water jar (hydria) of the 6th century B.C.

The Greek myths about the creation contain many non-Greek elements, assimilated from the non-Greek inhabitants of the country or from other parts, and they are closely similar to other myths, particularly Hittite. The sky-god Zeus is thoroughly Greek, yet he too can be paralleled in other cultures.

Zeus was connected with the weather, notably thunder and lightning, and also with the fertility of the soil – which largely depended on rainfall. However, he was much more than that. As the supreme god, he was connected with all human activities; Aeschylus called him 'the air, earth and sky; everything, and more than that'. Belief in a supreme sky god is so common as to be almost universal; in some religions, he becomes the Creator.

Zeus is usually portrayed in Greek art as a magnificent, bearded figure of a man, past his youth but still in his prime. In spite of being involved in some absurd and some silly incidents (mostly late inventions however), he remains always a grand and imposing figure. Often he is holding his thunderbolt, an object resembling more modern guided weapons, occasionally shown with lightning flashing from each end. Another weapon is his aegis (shield) which, when shaken, strikes terror into an enemy.

Many of the stories in which Zeus is the central character are concerned with his love affairs. These were both complicated and numerous. The Greeks were monogamous, and it was therefore fitting that Zeus should have but one wife; conveniently, she might represent the mother goddess of old, particularly in her aspect of Earth, but Hera, the consort of Zeus, is not perhaps a very satisfactory representative.

Hera was an important goddess at Argos, where the remains of her temple may still be seen, but she was also the daughter of Cronos and Gaea, and therefore the sister of Zeus. (Classical Greeks were sometimes troubled by all this incest, but their ancestors probably took these relationships less literally). Although she appears in various aspects in mythology, Hera is generally rather unsympathetic, even shrewish, though it must be said that as wife of Zeus she had a lot to put up with.

Zeus had a number of previous, or alternative, consorts, many of whom represent a union of Sky (Zeus) and Earth. They also included Metis (Wisdom), whom Zeus swallowed for the same reason as his father swallowed his children (by swallowing the mother, Zeus saved himself the trouble of swallowing each child individually). Metis was pregnant when swallowed and the result was that Athena, Zeus' favourite daughter, was born from her father's head. Being born from the union of Might and Wisdom, she was a goddess of formidable powers. Athena, rather than Hera, probably represents a powerful native goddess who had to be incorporated on equal terms with the sky god.

Zeus' other consorts included Demeter, the goddess of corn, again a very suitable union. Persephone, who became the mate of Hades (and, in one version, also of her father Zeus), was the product of this union. After Demeter came Mnemosyne (Memory), and from that union were born the nine Muses. Apollo and Artemis were the offspring of Zeus' union with Leto, like Mnemosyne, one of the female Titans.

All of these were more or less regular unions. But Zeus also had many irregular affairs, usually with mortal girls. As so many aristocratic families in Greece maintained that they were of part-divine descent, Zeus was – retrospectively as it were – kept very busy. Many of the Greek heroes (Heracles, Perseus, etc.) were descended from

A marble statue, now in the Archaeological Museum, Istanbul, of Tyche, one of the Fates (Moirai), the daughters of Night, who in Hesiod are abstract figures. Tyche is most reasonably identified as Fortune, good or bad, and was later the centre of a flourishing cult. The Romans knew her as Fortuna.

these extra-marital affairs of Zeus, which he used to undertake in a variety of ingenious disguises.

Having defeated the Titans, reached agreement with his brothers over the division of the universe, and provided himself with a wife, it remained for Zeus to determine his relations with mankind. His attitude towards men was seldom better than ambivalent, and at this stage hostile. Fortunately, men possessed an impressive champion in Prometheus, the cunning Titan who had supported Zeus in the war between the gods and the Titans but subsequently incurred the Thunderer's wrath.

The Nine Muses depicted in relief on a Roman sarcophagus. The Muses were the daughters of Zeus and Mnemosyne (Memory), a female Titan. The Muses could inspire writers and artists. They might also take away the gifts of a poet who was too boastful. This happened to Thamyris, who unwisely declared that he could sing better than they.

Punishment of the Titans. Atlas, left, supports the heavens; the chained Prometheus is attacked by the eagle which eats his liver. A 6th-century black-figure kylix (a shallow bowl on a stem).

The origin of men was explained in a number of ways. In some stories, men were created by Zeus as companions for his son Aeacus, who was alone on the island of Aegina, with no one to talk to but ants; Zeus obligingly turned the ants into men. In another version of the story, Zeus caused men to grow directly out of the earth, and this is much closer to the myths, found in Asia Minor and other parts as well as Greece, in which mankind springs direct from Earth—men and gods thus sharing a common origin.

Another account says that men were first made by Prometheus himself and his less clever brother, Epimetheus, or that the two brother Titans put the finishing touches to work begun by the gods deep in

An incident during the battle between the Olympians and the Giants, from an amphora now in Paris. Athena, attended by her usual owl, despatches the giant Enceladus.

the earth. Animals were made at the same time. Unfortunately, the job of equipping these creatures with abilities that would let them survive was entrusted to Epimetheus, who made a mess of things by giving all the most desirable qualities—speed, strength, etc.—to the animals, so that he had nothing left for man. At this point he called in his wiser brother, Prometheus, who evened things up by taking (only later sources say stealing) fire from the abode of Zeus as a gift for man.

This annoyed Zeus who, moreover, had other reasons for resenting Prometheus. The Titan knew a secret potentially disastrous for Zeus, but refused to reveal it. The secret concerned Thetis the Nereid. (The Nereids were the offspring of Nereus, the chief Water-god until eclipsed by Poseidon.) Thetis' offspring were destined to overthrow their father, as Zeus had overthrown Cronos and Cronos had overthrown Uranus. Zeus knew that he was likely to be overthrown in turn unless he could discover the identity of the mother destined to bear the rebel. Prometheus knew, but would not tell, and he further angered Zeus by playing a trick on him, again to the advantage of his favourites, men.

A sacrificial ox was to be shared between the gods and men. Prometheus was in charge of the butchery, and he placed all the good meat in the stomach while making a larger and more attractive parcel, wrapped in glistening fat, of the bones. Then he offered Zeus a choice. Zeus took the better-looking bundle and, to his anger, found he had the bones. Most of those who repeated the story say that Zeus really knew which parcel contained the meat, but in their eagerness not to make Zeus look foolish they do not explain why he therefore chose the bones. Anyway, from that time forth, when animals were sacrificed to the gods, the bones were put on the altar and the meat eaten at a feast. A better illustration of the practical value of a myth would be hard to find.

Zeus sought vengeance on Prometheus and on man and his plan was drastic. He invented women.

The effects were disastrous; at least, that is how it appears in

This elegant 5th-century vase shows the first woman, Pandora (right), who according to this artist apparently emerged from the earth after being fashioned by Hephaestus (with mallet). Hermes (in winged helmet) taught her guile. On the left, Zeus looks on.

Hesiod who, however, was no lover of women. There are other stories of how woman originated – she sprang from the earth, like man, or she was made by Prometheus – but it is unlikely that Hesiod's version was invented by him.

The basic article was fashioned by Hephaestus – the blacksmith-god from whose forge, in some versions, Prometheus had taken fire for man. She was decorated by Athena, and endowed with charm by Aphrodite. Finally, Hermes added the finishing touches by imbuing the lovely creature with treachery. She was named Pandora, 'All Gifts' (the name suggests an earth goddess).

Hermes the messenger delivered the attractive package, not to Prometheus, but to his simpler brother, Epimetheus. Prometheus had warned his brother to have nothing to do with any gifts sent by Zeus, but Epimetheus forgot the warning and did not see the evil concealed by beauty.

Until this time, man had lived an untroubled existence, free of disease and evil. But Pandora had with her, or came across (it is not clear where it came from) a vessel containing all the evils of the world. Out of curiosity, she opened it, and they all flew out, infecting the world with the evils, sickness and sorrow that have afflicted men ever since. Only Hope, beneath the rim of the vessel, did not escape, which Zeus had intended.

On Prometheus, Zeus also inflicted a terrible punishment. The fire-giver was borne away by Hephaestus and two of the mighty children of Styx to a high peak in the Caucasus, and there chained to a rock. Every day an eagle came and fed on his liver, but during the freezing mountain nights the flesh was restored so that the torture went on for ever.

So Prometheus suffered for his help to man for a long, long time. However, the punishment proved not to be eternal, and he was eventually released. The tormenting eagle was shot by Heracles, and Zeus released the prisoner in exchange for his valuable information about Thetis the Nereid, just in time to prevent Zeus from marrying her. (She subsequently married Peleus, a mortal, which ended the danger). At this time the wise centaur, Chiron, instructor of Achilles, was suffering from a wound he had received when Heracles accidentally shot him with one of his poisoned arrows. As an Immortal, Chiron could not die, yet he wished to do so to end his suffering. Zeus therefore allowed him to bestow his immortality on Prometheus, and Chiron gratefully embraced death.

Prometheus, as the benefactor of man, is one of the most attractive figures in Greek mythology. Aeschylus made him the central figure of two of his plays (though only one has survived) in which Prometheus represents man's struggle against Fate.

The Olympians

One reason for the complicated relationships of the divine family in Greek mythology is the mingling of different religious traditions—the necessity to incorporate new gods with those already established. Thus, the affairs of Zeus may be largely explained as the assimilation of local goddesses with the Olympian family. It also explains why many of the gods appear to have more than two parents. Many of the names of Zeus' lovers suggest that they were not mere individuals. Europa is one example; another is Leda, whose name in Asia Minor meant simply 'woman'.

In the myth, Leda was the daughter of a king of Aetolia and the wife of a king of Sparta, Tyndareus. She used to bathe in the river Eurotas, and one day encountered a swan, which seemed friendly. The swan was Zeus (birds were often associated with divinity), and union inevitably resulted. Three children resulted, Castor and Pollux, and Helen, over whom the Trojan War was to be fought. Helen was hatched from an egg, a beautiful blue egg, but not every version of the myth says that the egg was actually laid by Leda. It may have been the result of a previous union between Zeus and Nemesis, daughter of Night and symbol of fateful retribution, who seems a very suitable mother for Helen. However, the egg certainly came into Leda's possession, by one means or another, so that she was responsible for hatching it even if she did not lay it.

Zeus' frequent amorous exploits made it inevitable that his consort, Hera, should turn into a shrew, but originally she must have been a rather different figure. Her name could be a feminine version of 'hero', and in Argos she was no doubt a powerful mother goddess—as most of the female deities once were. She is associated with some of the heroes, including Heracles, whose name means 'glory of Hera', and Jason, although as the jealous wife of Zeus, she appears in later myth as resentful of Heracles because he was an extra-marital son of Zeus. Whatever she may have been originally—earth goddess, moon goddess and so on—she became the goddess, primarily, of marriage and child-bearing. However, her own children were few and comparatively insignificant.

According to one story, Hera chose the young Zeus as her future husband, and seduced him with a love potion provided by Aphrodite. Another story tells how Zeus determined to have Hera, and enticed her into a compromising position while disguised as a cuckoo.

The tales of the home life of Zeus and Hera must come from a relatively early period because of the rough manners displayed by Zeus, which Homer's heroes would never have stooped to. Zeus, indeed, was ready to use violence against her, even hurling his thunderbolts at her. Once, when Zeus had been particularly difficult,

Left:
The marriage of Zeus and Hera. From the 6th-century temple of Hera at Selinus in Sicily.

Io, in the form of a cow, was watched by Argus the hundred-eyed (many of them in very odd places) on the orders of Hera, who sought to frustrate Zeus' lust for Io. But Zeus sent Hermes to kill Argus. Attic red-figure amphora. (Greek vases, so abundant a source of pictorial information on mythology and culture generally, were of course utilitarian in purpose. Experts classify them in many more-or-less technical ways. The commonest forms are: *amphora*, a high-shouldered jar with a neck, for storing wine or oil; *krater*, a wide-mouthed, bulky vessel for mixing water and wine; *hydria*, or water jar, which often has a pouring handle plus two handles in the horizontal plane for lifting the jar on to the shoulder, for carrying. There are many other types, including plain jugs and cups. The black-figure technique–figures in black silhouette–dates from the 7th century B.C. and originated in Corinth. Red-figure (on a black ground) is primarily associated with Attica, and began in the late 6th century. Many individual artists are known, though not always by name.)

Hera combined with other gods to imprison Zeus with unbreakable thongs, removing his thunderbolts to a safe distance. It looked as though Zeus might be overthrown, but Thetis the Nereid helped him escape and, to punish Hera, Zeus hung her from the sky by her wrists, attaching heavy weights to her ankles. He kept her in that painful position until the gods promised not to rebel against him in future.

In art, Hera is frequently portrayed as a dignified, mature woman, but she was as capable of arousing Zeus as any comely young woman (though sometimes requiring the help of Aphrodite's girdle), and in one of the most famous stories in which she appears she is a contestant in an Olympian beauty contest. That incident led, indirectly, to the outbreak of the Trojan War.

Argos, with the citadel of Mycenae in the foreground. Hera was an ancient, pre-Hellenic goddess and Argos was the centre of her worship – she was often called Argive Hera. Later, in organised religion, she became the wife of Zeus.

Opposite, top :
This magnificent bronze figure now in the National Museum, Athens, was recovered from the sea in 1928. It was at first thought to be Zeus, but the prevailing opinion now is that it is Poseidon, although he looks sleeker and calmer than usual.

Bottom :
A domestic scene on Olympus: Poseidon (with trident) and Amphitrite, Zeus and Hera, with Ganymede attending them.

It will be remembered that Zeus had two brothers with whom he ruled the universe, Poseidon, who ruled the sea, or rather the waters, fresh and salt, and Hades, who ruled (and gave his name to) the Underworld. Poseidon may have felt that Zeus had much the best of the bargain, for although it never came to a full-scale war, Poseidon often appears critical of, and hostile to, Zeus.

As god of the sea, Poseidon was naturally important to the sea-going Greeks; he was often worshipped and he appeared in many myths, though he remained a minor figure by comparison with Zeus. Besides governing the seas, he was frequently connected with horses (one of his titles was *Hippios*), and this is interesting because it suggests that Poseidon was a very early figure, probably going back to those who introduced the horse into Greece, and that his maritime associations came later. The meaning of his name is uncertain, but it appears to mean 'husband of Da', Da being an earth goddess, who may well have been connected with Demeter. Poseidon certainly had an affair with Demeter, the circumstances of which tend to corroborate the belief that he was once the god of horses and as such took the form of a horse himself.

At the time when Poseidon courted Demeter, she was lamenting the loss of her daughter, Persephone, carried off by Hades, and wanted nothing to do with Poseidon. To escape him, she turned herself into a mare, and hid among a herd of horses. Poseidon spotted her trick however, and turned himself into a stallion in order to mate with her; their offspring were a nymph and a wild horse, Arion, which became the property of Adrastus, King of Argos. Demeter was enraged, and her aspect of Demeter as Fury dates from Poseidon's shabby trick. The story of the rape of Demeter, incidentally, has an almost exact parallel in early Indian mythology, from which it probably derives.

The temple of Hera at Olympia, dating from the beginning of the 7th century B.C. The original building was wooden, and it was replaced by stone over a period of years, showing variations in style.

Opposite :
Caenis was a Lapith woman whose charms provoked Poseidon to sieze and ravish her. Afterwards he offered her a wish, and she promptly demanded a change of sex. So she became Caeneus— and Poseidon also made him invulnerable. But in the fight between Lapiths and Centaurs Caeneus was hammered into the ground by his foes. Bronze relief, 7th century B.C.

Demeter was by no means Poseidon's only passing fancy, and his sexual behaviour caused as much trouble for his sea goddess, Amphitrite the Nereid, as Zeus' did for Hera. Indeed, Poseidon is in many ways like a rather inferior Zeus, usually portrayed as a similarly impressive, mature male figure, clasping his trident, but often rougher and more violent than his more successful brother. His wife, Amphitrite, is similarly reminiscent of Hera. She was originally relucant to marry Poseidon and one probably rather late myth recounts how she hid from him and was revealed to Poseidon by the dolphin which, in gratitude, Poseidon placed among the stars as a constellation.

Poseidon and Amphitrite had several children, but the only one who appears frequently in mythology, and then only as a minor character, is Triton, the merman, with his 'wreathed horn'. He is barely an individual, and is often merely one of a race of Tritons. Poseidon himself had many children, by and large rather a rough lot and many of them in non-human form. Polyphemus, the one-eyed giant, was a fairly typical example. Persons wishing to possess a tough political image often claimed descent from Poseidon.

The best-known story of Amphitrite's jealousy concerned Scylla, daughter of Phorcys and Hecate. When she heard that Poseidon was courting Scylla, Amphitrite threw magic herbs into the water where Scylla bathed which turned her into a monster with six heads – and those the heads of dogs. She became a threat to sailors, catching and eating those who ventured near her cave, which was said to be located opposite the Straits of Messina. On the other side of the straits was another sea-monster, of a different kind but no less deadly, named Charybdis, and sailors trying to avoid the one often fell into the clutches of the other.

Poseidon appears in several myths as an aspirant, usually disappointed, for territorial sovereignty. The stories must have grown from political rivalries, although it is not always clear exactly what reality the myth reflects. The best-known of these stories, which concerns the city of Athens, may stem from the conflict between a native earth goddess of the Minoan type and the warlike god of sea-going invaders.

The rivals for dominion in Attica (the country of Athens) were Poseidon and Athena. Arbitration was arranged, in one version by Zeus himself, and it was agreed that the winner should be the one who gave the Athenians the more valuable gift. Poseidon struck the rock of the Acropolis with his trident, and a salt-water spring immediately issued from the rock. The mark of his trident can be seen today in an opening in the porch of the Erectheum. Another version says that Poseidon's gift was the horse, which would certainly have been more useful than a well of sea-water. However, Athena won the contest by raising an olive tree beside the spring, which was judged the more useful innovation. (The cultivated olive was probably introduced to Greece from Libya, and Athena was identified with certain North African cults).

Zeus abducting Ganymede, a Trojan princeling of great beauty who became cup-bearer to the gods. The game cock carried by Ganymede would have been given him by Zeus: it was the traditional lover's gift. A terracotta figure of the 5th century B.C.

Poseidon, who had originally proposed settling the matter by single combat, was enraged by the decision and, as he frequently did when angry, called up a flood. Peace was eventually restored, though at some cost to the Athenians. To still Poseidon's anger, the women of Athens were not allowed to vote (in the recent contest, all the goddesses had supported Athena against Poseidon). Although Athena remained supreme at Athens, Poseidon was a much-revered god there.

There are a number of other stories of territorial disputes involving Poseidon. He contested Troezen with Athena, and at Zeus' command agreed to share the city with her, an arrangement that pleased neither. He tried to claim various other places, including Corinth, but was everywhere denied. He even tried to gain Argos from Hera, where he let loose another flood, accusing the Olympians of being biased against him. Zeus then appointed independent judges – three River-gods – who might indeed have been expected to favour Poseidon. But they gave the verdict to Hera, and Poseidon thereupon dried up their rivers, which since then have never flowed in summer.

Zeus' other brother, Hades, is a more remote figure than Poseidon. As lord of the Underworld, he is naturally rather grim, but the Greeks had no neurotic fears about death and hell, and Hades is not a figure of evil. He has little in common with Satan in Christian mythology. In art he is portrayed as just and serene, similar to Zeus but grimmer.

The house or kingdom of Hades is generally thought of as the Underworld, but it is sometimes located in the far west, beyond the place where Atlas stands supporting the vault of heaven. Various places were locally regarded as entrances to hell. Beyond the waters is the Plain of Asphodel, a kind of limbo where the departed wait in ghostlike form, except for those favoured individuals who go to Elysium, the archetypal Land of the Blessed, where all is happiness and light. Elysium is separated from Tartaros by a river.

The wicked go to Tartaros, where Odysseus observed various horrid and perpetual ordeals being undergone by those who had been so unwise as to offend the gods. Theseus spent some time in Tartaros, imprisoned in a chair from which he could not move, for his attempt to abduct Persephone, Hades' queen. There are various figures in authority in the Underworld. Hades himself seldom appears as a judge of the dead, and that function is often fulfilled by three former kings, Minos, his brother Rhadamanthys, who ruled in Elysium, and Aeacus. Other, more disturbing presences in the Underworld were the Erinyes, or Furies.

The three Furies were the offspring of Gaea, when the blood of the castrated Uranus fell upon her. They probably represent feelings of guilt aroused by breaking sacred laws. They were just, but fearful avengers of social crime, on earth and in the Underworld, and had a hideous appearance, with heads of dogs, hair of snakes and wings of bats. It was unwise to speak of them directly, and therefore they were often referred to by a highly euphemistic nickname, Eumenides, 'the Kindly Ones' – an appealingly hypocritical metaphor adopted by Aeschylus for one of his plays in the *Oresteia* and by Anthony Powell for a novel in his *Music of Time* series which deals with the coming of war.

The Underworld in Greek mythology, even more than other conceptions, is made confusing by the mixture of different beliefs that are involved in it. In classical times it was still possible to hold contrary opinions on what happened to the dead. The frontier of the Underworld is water, usually the River Styx ('hateful'), which has to be crossed by a ferry. The ferryman is an ugly old man, Charon, who must be paid for his services; hence the money put into the mouth

of a corpse. The Underworld has another sentinel-figure in the fearsome, many-headed hound Cerberus, the son of the monsters Geryon and Typhon, who does not fit in very well with the idea of the entrance being formed by a river. But the Underworld was often described in a literal manner as the 'House of Hades', and there a watchdog would obviously be suitable.

Hades himself, perhaps not surprisingly, figures as the central character in only a few myths, and they are generally rather obscure. There is one notable exception, the story of how he acquired his queen, the redemptive goddess of the dead, Persephone.

Persephone was the daughter of the corn-goddess, Demeter, by Zeus. She was exceedingly beautiful and carefully guarded by her mother in, some say, Sicily. One day she was playing in the fields with Artemis and Athena and other suitable companions when her attention was caught by a lovely flower, usually identified as a narcissus. As she reached to pick it, the earth suddenly yawned wide, and from it sprang the golden chariot of Hades with its mighty steeds. The god of the Underworld seized the maiden with the rosebud face and carried her off.

Demeter, Persephone and Triptolemus. A 5th-century marble relief found at Eleusis. Triptolemus is being invested with the fruits of the harvest, in preparation for his agricultural mission to the world.

An interesting portrait in terracotta of an Earth goddess, either Demeter or her daughter, Persephone. From Delphi.

Zeus had given permission for Hades to take Persephone, but her mother had not been consulted. Hearing the cries of her distressed daughter, Demeter flew to her aid, but could find no trace of her. Distraught, she searched for her all over the world. Hecate, the companion of Persephone, had also heard her cries, but did not know who had taken her, though Helios, the Sun, who sees everything, finally revealed that Zeus was behind the disappearance, and that Persephone had been carried off by Hades.

Helios suggested that things might be worse. After all, he pointed out, Hades was a great king in his own country. But Demeter was not to be consoled and, in rage against Zeus, she left Olympus and went to live among men. Meanwhile, famine overtook the world, as without Demeter the crops would not grow.

It was during her wanderings that Demeter attempted without success to evade the lecherous Poseidon by turning herself into a mare. Soon after this unpleasant episode, she came, still in disguise, to Eleusis, where she was kindly treated by King Celeus and Queen Metaneira, and agreed to become the nurse of their baby son, Demophoon. The wise maiden, Iambe, by her jokes relieved the goddess somewhat of her intense gloom, and the baby Demophoon prospered exceedingly in Demeter's care. Secretly, she prepared the child for immortality, which involved exposing him to the flames of a fire. One evening Queen Metaneira saw this process and promptly had hysterics, thinking that Demeter was killing her son. This ruined the treatment and made Demeter, usually a gentle creature as Greek goddesses go, extremely angry. She resumed the form of a goddess, and demanded that a temple should be built to her at Eleusis and that priests should be presented to be instructed by her in the manner of worship that would best honour her. King Celeus ordered the temple to be built, and there Demeter took up residence, still refusing to associate with the gods.

Thus Eleusis became the chief centre of the worship of Demeter; indeed, the festival of Demeter Thesmophoria ('bringer of treasures') became the most popular in all Greek religion.

Zeus had felt a little reluctant to endorse Hades' desire for Persephone in the very beginning, knowing that Demeter would not accept Hades as son-in-law, and his fears had been borne out by the state of the world when Demeter stopped fulfilling her function as goddess of the cornfield. The oxen drew the plough in vain; the sowed seeds did not sprout. So Zeus attempted to end Demeter's self-imposed exile. He sent many messengers to Eleusis to persuade the goddess to return, but she would not relent. The earth would never know another harvest until she was reunited with Persephone.

Nothing remained except to bring Persephone back from the

Below :
An Attic black-figure amphora with a scene showing the birth of Athena, fully armed (including her Gorgon's head shield), from the head of Zeus. In the Museum of Fine Arts, Boston.

Bottom :
Perseus takes off with Medusa's head safely stashed in his satchel. Athena, the friend of heroes, is in attendance.

The Acropolis in Athens, the most-visited classical site, crowned by the Parthenon, with the Propylea at the left. The great temple was dedicated to Athena Parthenos (the virgin), while in front of it stood a lofty statue of her as Athena Polias (protectress of the city).

Underworld. The delicate mission was undertaken by Hermes, the messenger god, who found Persephone unreconciled to her new abode. Black-haired Hades was willing to let her go at Zeus' command, but before she went he made her eat the seeds of a pomegranate, which would compel her to return. Another story says that Persephone picked the pomegranate from Hades' garden, but a minor Underworld figure, Askalaphos, saw her eat it and reported the fact to Hades. Demeter later turned Askalaphos into an owl and confined him in a hole in the ground, from which he was later released by Heracles.

Hermes harnessed the horses to the golden chariot, saw Persephone safely into a seat, and drove at great speed to Eleusis, ignoring ravines and precipices on the way. At Eleusis there was a joyful reunion of mother and daughter, dampened only when Persephone replied to her mother's question as to whether she had taken any food in the house of Hades that she had indeed eaten the pomegranate seeds.

However, the situation was not too bad. Zeus ordained that Persephone should spend one-third of the year with Hades and two-thirds with her mother and the rest of the gods on Olympus. Demeter agreed to let the corn grow again, and soon the earth was covered with grass and flowers.

Persephone, whose earlier name was Kore ('maiden'), besides being the queen of the Underworld, was also associated with her mother as a goddess of fruitfulness, and may once have been merely an aspect of Demeter. The season that she spends with Hades is winter.

One late version of the myth says that Demeter did not merely *restore* the growth of corn when Persephone was released, she *introduced* it. The agent of Demeter who spread knowledge of agriculture around the world was said to be a son of King Celeus of Eleusis, Triptolemos. In this version, it was Triptolemos who first recognized the goddess and told her the fate of her daughter, and the gift of corn was his reward. Demeter provided him with a chariot drawn by winged dragons in order to assist the spread of agriculture.

Demeter also figures in a large number of local myths, many of them bearing a close resemblance to the Eleusinian story. Many places claimed to be the site of Hades' emergence from the Underworld to kidnap Persephone.

Demeter was responsible for turning several ill-behaved people into animals. There is, for instance, a type of lizard named after one of her victims. He was a bad-mannered youth named Askalabos, who laughed at the way Demeter, in a moment of exhaustion during her search for Persephone, eagerly swallowed a drink containing meal. She threw the drink at him, and he turned into a lizard bearing the marks of the meal on his skin.

An equally unpleasant fate overtook Erysichthon when, in order to get timber to build a banqueting hall, he cut down the trees in a grove sacred to Demeter. Disguised as one of her own priestesses, Demeter warned him to stop, but when he did not she remarked that he might as well continue as he would have need of a banqueting hall in future. Erysichthon went home and had a meal, but found he was still hungry. The more he ate the hungrier he became. He grew thinner and thinner while eating more and more. He ended up a desperate beggar, eating filth from the gutters in a vain effort to assuage the pangs of ravenous hunger. The element of truth in the story is disturbing: man has impoverished many fertile regions by his greedy destruction of trees.

The 4th-century temple of Athena Polias at Priene, Turkey. The goddess's protection was invoked throughout the Greek world.

A relief from Olympia of Heracles, watched by Athena, clearing out the Augean Stables.

Of all the female deities on Olympus, the most formidable was surely Pallas Athena. There are practically no recorded instances of the kind of petty revenges, which other gods often gave way to, associated with Athena, and no disreputable amorous exploits; indeed, she had no husband and no children. Probably, this reputation for nobility and chastity is partly the effect of Athenian propaganda. Some of the myths concerning Athena show signs of having been 'cleaned up' to exalt the goddess of Athens.

Athena was a formidable figure from the first moment, when she sprang, fully armed and shouting her war cry, from the head of Zeus, after Hephaestus had released her by cleaving her father's head in order to cure what was becoming an extremely painful headache. (The cure, one might think, might have been as dangerous as the cause, if the patient had been anyone but Zeus).

There are other stories of her birth. In one, she was the daughter of Pallas (the word can be masculine or feminine, and means a powerful youth), who later assaulted her but was defeated by his warlike daughter. Another candidate as Athena's father is one of the Cyclops, who is said to have made Metis pregnant before Zeus swallowed her.

It is generally agreed that Athena is a pre-Greek goddess. An early name for her suggests an origin connected with water, and places where she was worshipped support this idea.

Athena was a goddess of war, and in art she is normally portrayed in armour, but she was also the goddess of crafts and skills and, locally, of children, of work and so on. (All the major deities had numerous surnames which identified them in various different aspects at different times and places). She was Zeus' favourite daughter and the most popular deity in many parts of Greece after Zeus himself. The finest temple in Greece was dedicated to her – the temple of the Virgin at Athens, better known as the Parthenon.

Hephaestus came nearer than anyone else to taking the virginity of Athena. It is said that he demanded her as a reward for assisting in her birth, or alternatively as payment for the armour he made for her in the Trojan war. She was unwilling; but Hephaestus was told by Poseidon – a frequent opponent of Athena, as has already appeared – that Athena was actually eager to be taken by force. Thus emboldened, Hephaestus attempted to make love to her, but she fought him off (or, in another version, simply vanished) and the seed of Hephaestus fell upon the Earth. The fertile Mother Earth (Gaea) promptly conceived, yet she was no more willing than Athena to give birth to the child of Hephaestus. Athena volunteered to take responsibility for the child, which turned out to be a boy, Erichthonius, and she gave him to the daughter of King Cecrops to look after.

Cecrops, himself a son of Gaea, was the legendary first king of Athens. He was not a man, having serpents for legs, but he was an important reformer, who was said to have been responsible for instituting monogamy and for realising that children have fathers as well as mothers. His wife, and his eldest daughter, who took charge of Erichthonius, were named Aglauros, a name sometimes associated with Athena herself. The child was confined in a basket – some say he was also a serpent, or part-serpent – and the daughters of Cecrops were forbidden to open the basket. Needless to say, they disobeyed. They went mad, and jumped to their deaths from the Acropolis.

At this time Athena was approaching Athens with a great rock, which she proposed adding to the fortifications of the Acropolis. A crow told her the sad news, whereupon she dropped the rock, now to be seen as Mount Lycabettus, and banned all crows from the Acropolis in future, at the same time turning them black; for crows

had previously been white birds. Erichthonius, however, grew up to become king of Athens, where he furthered the worship of Athena, whom some took to be his mother (a very natural conclusion in view of Athena's close protection of him after the deaths of Cecrops' daughters), and invented the four-horse chariot (a means of transport also credited to several other inventors however, including Athena).

As the protectress of skilled crafts, Athena was especially concerned with spinning and weaving–women's work in ancient Greece. A story related by Ovid (not a sound guide to authentic Greek myth) is interesting because it suggests an inter-city economic rivalry, though Athena's actions are not typical of her.

There was a skilful princess of Lydia, named Arachne, who unwisely boasted that she could spin better than Athena herself. The goddess appeared to Arachne in the guise of an old woman and advised her to be more modest, and when Arachne ignored this advice Athena challenged her to a contest. Arachne produced a fine piece of work which Athena, either because she was annoyed at the evidence of Arachne's skill or because the design the Lydian princess had chosen illustrated in a satirical manner the private life of the gods (rather an Ovidian touch, one suspects), tore into pieces. Arachne, in anger or fear, hanged herself from a rafter, but Athena turned her into a spider which, though an unpleasant fate for a princess, allowed her to go on living, by climbing up the rope, and to go on spinning. (In modern zoological language, all spiders are Arachnids).

Athena, although the daughter of Zeus, seems to belong to the older generation of deities on Olympus, like Poseidon and Demeter. Apollo and his sister Artemis belong to the second generation.

Apollo is the golden youth, beautiful and strong, whose charms are such that he can, literally in Apollo's case, get away with murder. Indeed, Apollo shows many of the characteristics of a juvenile delinquent, though he becomes respectable later. Although the beautiful young god is a common figure in mythology, it seems fairly certain that Apollo arrived late in Greece, and was brought by nomadic invaders: one of his duties was the care of flocks and herds. In art Apollo is invariably a splendid young man. He usually carries a lyre or a bow, music and archery being pursuits he patronizes, and is sometimes accompanied by the bird sacred to him, the raven.

Leto gives birth to Apollo, the scene depicted in low relief on the neck of a pithos (a large, cask-like vessel) from Thebes in the Archaic period.

Leto and her famous children, Apollo (with his lyre) and Artemis. Attic red-figure jar now in the British Museum.

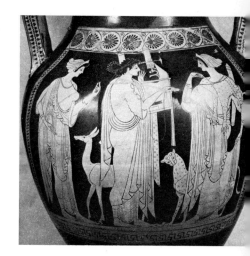

The temple of Aphaea on the island of Aegina. Aphaea was a local goddess who eventually became assimilated to Athena.

One of Zeus' loves was Leto, a female Titan, whom he made pregnant with twins. But Hera's wrath was aroused and her vengeance pursued Leto. For that reason, or alternatively because of their fear of the formidable god that Leto was about to give birth to, no land would receive her. Eventually she made her way to Ortygia, near Delos, two islands that at that time floated in the sea. There she gave birth to Artemis, who helped her mother cross over to Delos and there delivered her brother, Apollo. Like his sister, Apollo was precocious. He called for weapons at the age of four days. They were promptly supplied by Hephaestus, and Apollo departed to seek the serpent Python, one of Hera's instruments in her persecution of Leto, and kill him. Python fled to Delphi, an oracle of Mother Earth, where Apollo killed him in the sacred precincts. (The story no doubt symbolizes a take-over of the religious cult at Delphi, which became the chief centre, after Delos, for the worship of Apollo). However, Mother Earth protested to Zeus about this act of sacrilege, and Apollo was ordered to undergo rites of purification. He showed no particular anxiety to obey, but eventually did so. He took up residence at Delphi where the Pythoness (priestess) became his oracle; it is said that Apollo had learned the secret of prophecy from the nature god, Pan. Not much is left of the temple at Delphi now. The best-known remains are those of the Tholos, whose three standing columns were re-erected in recent times. This was in the sanctuary of Athena, who, with Dionysus, was also represented at Delphi.

Once Apollo was established at Delphi, Leto made her way there, accompanied by Artemis, but while praying in a sacred grove, the mother of Apollo was assaulted by the 900-foot giant, Tityus. Hearing her cries, Apollo came to the rescue, and the arrows of Apollo and Artemis disabled or killed Tityus. The giant went to Tartaros, where he was tied to the ground while two vultures perpetually ate his liver. (The liver was believed to be the seat of desire, and that was why it was the organ usually attacked in such myths).

One of the best-known, if least attractive, of the stories about Apollo relates his rivalry with Marsyas, a satyr. Satyrs were semi-human, semi-bestial creatures of the woods, associated with Dionysus, lustful and fond of dancing; though Marsyas appears a more cultured creature.

The goddess Athena was playing the double flute, which some say she invented, when she noticed other goddesses hiding their laughter as they listened. Their humour was provoked by the curious faces Athena made as she blew, and, disgusted with this effect, she discarded the flute beside a stream. There Marsyas found it, and although Athena was displeased, so much so that she gave him a beating for not leaving the flute alone, he became an expert player – perhaps because the flute was inspired by the memory of Athena's divine music. Those who heard Marsyas playing said that Apollo himself could not make better music on his lyre. The ominous result was the arrangement of a contest to judge who made the most beautiful music. The Muses were to judge, and the winner was to inflict on the loser any punishment he liked.

To Apollo's wrath, the Muses found both instruments so beautiful that they could not decide between them. He insisted on another round in which the contestants would sing as well. As it was impossible to sing while playing the pipes, Apollo won, and the punishment he inflicted on Marsyas was to be flayed alive.

Apollo's supremacy in the sphere of music was confirmed by another contest, in which he defeated Pan. King Midas, one of the judges, unwisely voted for Pan, whereupon Apollo gave him donkey's ears. (These contests may reflect the change, among the well-to-do, from wind instruments to stringed instruments).

Apollo never had a wife, though he had many children as a result of illicit affairs. In spite of his attractiveness, he was not especially successful in love. The laurel wreath he is often shown wearing is a reminder of one of his failures. The nymph Daphne, daughter of an

Below :
Apollo, most glamorous of gods. This impressive head belonged to a sculptured scene on the west pediment of the temple of Zeus at Olympia, in which Apollo intervenes in the battle between the Centaurs and the Lapiths. It dates from 460 B.C.

Below, left :
Apollo and Artemis arrive at Delphi just in time to prevent Tityus raping their mother, Leto.

The view from Delphi, with the road leading down to the Gulf of Corinth, once travelled by many hopeful inquirers of the oracle.

Mount Parnassus with a mantle of snow. In the Greek story of the Deluge Prometheus warned his son Deucalion, king of Phthia, of the wrath of Zeus and the floods that were coming: like Noah, Deucalion built an ark, which came to rest on Parnassus when the waters subsided.

Arcadian river god, was desired by Apollo and by Leukippos, who disguised himself as a girl and joined the nymphs at play in order to approach her. But Apollo suggested that they should go bathing, and the shedding of clothes revealed Leukippos as an imposter. The enraged nymphs killed him; but the removal of his rival did not benefit Apollo, as Daphne did not want him either. He pursued her and had almost caught her when she was changed into a laurel tree, probably by Mother Earth, who took pity on her.

Of the many love stories in which Apollo is involved, one of the best-known concerned his love for a young man, Hyacinthus. (Homosexual love was not unusual in Greece; Zeus, for example, desired the beautiful youth Ganymede, and carried him off to become cup-bearer to the gods). In this case again, Apollo had rivals, Zephyros, the West wind, and Thamyris, a poet, who dropped out of the contest when he offended the Muses and was struck blind and dumb as a result.

One windy day, Apollo was teaching Hyacinthus how to throw the discus, when Zephyros snatched it with an angry gust and returned it so that it struck Hyacinthus and killed him. From his blood grew the flower named after him. (Other evidence suggests that Hyacinthus was no pretty boy but probably a local god connected with the crops; the myth may explain the absorption of the old, local cult of Hyacinthus by the Dorian Apollo).

In view of the violence of many of the myths of Apollo, it is easy to forget that to the Greeks he was a moral figure and patron of the arts and sciences, of music and medicine, and other worthy activities. By contrast, his sister Artemis who, as the Virgin Huntress, might be expected to cut a decidedly Amazonian figure, often appears rather feeble, certainly when compared with Hera or Athena. When she decided to take part in the Trojan war, for instance, Hera scoffed at her, took her weapons away from her, boxed her ears, and sent her crying back to Olympus. This is not typical and may be only Homer venting a personal dislike.

But besides her love of hunting, Artemis has more gentle interests. She is the protector of small children and young animals, and like Apollo has the power of healing, though she also has a habit of causing sudden death by a shot from her silver bow. 'Artemis' is a non-Greek name, and she may have been originally a mother goddess who, having no consort, or at least not one of any note, was changed into the Greek virgin goddess. At her temple at Ephesus, which became one of the wonders of the ancient world, she was worshipped as the giver of fertility, which supports the theory that she was originally a mother goddess. In classical literature she is a gracious and elegant goddess, and was so portrayed by classical artists.

Nevertheless, it was dangerous to offend Artemis, as the story of Actaeon shows. There are many versions of this myth, but the best-known is that Actaeon, a hunter, stumbled on Artemis accidentally as she was bathing. She turned him into a stag, and he was torn to death by his own hounds.

Artemis was always attended by nymphs, several of them famous as the subject of myths. One of them was Callisto (her name was also applied to Artemis herself, and possibly she was once identified with the goddess), who was seduced by Zeus disguised as Artemis herself. When Artemis discovered that Callisto was pregnant – a fact revealed by another bathing ritual, often a source of disaster where Artemis was concerned – she was so angry that she turned Callisto into a bear. Subsequently she was transferred to the sky, where she can still be seen in the form of Ursa Major (the Great Bear). Possibly, Artemis

Hyacinthus was loved by Apollo and also by Zephyrus, the west wind, here pursuing him.

61

herself was once thought of as a bear. At Athens, pre-pubescent
girls used to perform a dance in her honour; they were called bears
and wore saffron gowns representing, it has been suggested, the
bear's pelt.

Artemis was also responsible for the death of Orion, a gigantic but
beautiful son of Poseidon, whose father gave him the gift of walking
on the sea. He was a great hunter, with a wife called Side ('pomegranate') who was despatched to the Underworld after offending
Hera, and was probably a local variation of Persephone. Orion's
disposition was amorous, and among those he pursued were the
Pleiades, daughters of Atlas. Later, he visited Oenopion, 'the wine-
faced', in Chios, and fell for his host's daughter. Tired of waiting for
marriage, he raped her, whereupon Oenopion blinded him. A small
boy, sitting on his shoulder, guided him to the sunrise, where he
regained his sight and hurried back to Chios to have his revenge on
Oenopion. But Oenopion avoided him, and Artemis despatched
Orion with her arrows. Another version says that Orion tried to rape
Artemis, and she raised up a great scorpion which stung him to death.

A god who might have been expected to carry great weight in
Olympus was Hephaestus, the son of Zeus and Hera (though,
according to Hesiod, he was a spontaneous son of Hera, produced in
response to the birth of Athena). Hephaestus remained, however, a
minor figure. He was lame, a little slow-witted at times and occasionally the butt of the other gods' jokes.

Hephaestus came originally from Asia. He was a fire god, and
was chiefly worshipped in regions of volcanic activity, but in Greece
he was changed into a smith. He was not universally worshipped in
Greece; his cult was usually found in the larger towns, where crafts-
men like himself were most numerous. The beautiful temple in
Athens known as the Theseum, because of its sculptures celebrating
the deeds of Theseus, was dedicated to Hephaestus. He has always
been popular with artists, partly, no doubt, because his forge, with
the sparks flying and the Cyclops workmen scurrying around in the
background gloom, makes a challenging subject. As the divine metal
worker, he was certainly a useful member of the Olympian family,
making thunderbolts for Zeus, arrows for Artemis, and armour for
Achilles, whose mother, Thetis, had been his earliest benefactor.

For when Hephaestus was born, Hera was so repelled by his physical disability that she threw him from Olympus. He fell into the sea and was rescued by Thetis, who provided him with his first forge. He made such exquisite jewellery that he was eventually invited back to Olympus, though later – or possibly it is a different version of the first occasion – he was thrown out again, by Zeus, after he had intervened in a quarrel between his parents. He fell for a whole day, but landed safely on Lemnos.

Hephaestus sometimes got his own back. When he returned to Olympus after being thrown out by Hera, he brought with him a throne which, when Hera sat on it, held her immovably. It was necessary for Dionysus to get Hephaestus drunk in order to persuade him to release the goddess.

The wife of Hephaestus was Aphrodite, apparently an unsuitable match. Certainly Aphrodite thought so, but Zeus insisted on it. Aphrodite much preferred the virile Ares. When he learned from all-seeing Helios that he was being cuckolded, Hephaestus made an invisible net of bronze, which fell upon the bed and trapped the guilty lovers *in flagrante delicto*, whereupon the injured husband summoned the gods to witness the scene. They were amused, but Hephaestus spoke angrily of divorce, until Poseidon, in the uncharacteristic role of mediator, managed to pacify him. Although this story appears in Homer, it is clearly a comparatively late myth and appears to have no significance beyond entertainment.

Aphrodite herself was a more substantial figure than her husband (or her lover).

Opposite, top:
Hephaestus and his workmen making armour for Achilles, watched by Athena and Hera. From a Roman relief.

Bottom, left:
Hephaestus displays the finished armour to Athena. From a 5th-century bowl now in Berlin.

Bottom, right:
Orion running across the sea (represented by a wavy line and fishes). From an Etruscan bronze mirror-back.

A relief carving of the birth of Aphrodite from the sea, with handmaidens present to preserve the goddess' modesty.

The theatre at Ephesus, Turkey, which seated 24,000 people, with the Arcadian Way in the foreground. Artemis was the revered goddess of Ephesus: the Ephesians, as they made plain to St Paul, were in no doubt that their much envied wealth and prosperity was due to her patronage.

If the account given by Hesiod of her birth—from the sea-foam that arose when the genitals of Uranus were cast into it—is true, as her name, 'Foam-born', implies, then Aphrodite was older than Zeus himself. Yet the Goddess of Love is always a young goddess. Homer makes her a daughter of Zeus, by Dione, whose name is the feminine form of Zeus; she was probably an early Earth goddess. Originally, Aphrodite came from Asia, where many goddesses of her type were worshipped in different parts; she can be identified with Astarte or, in Babylonia, Ishtar.

Aphrodite is the goddess of both kinds of love, sexual love and the 'higher' love; she is the goddess of marriage and beauty. In various places she had other attributes also, and her association with Ares probably results from her aspect of war goddess in Cyprus and elsewhere. Sometimes she is the protector of mariners also. In early Greek art, she is a grand and stately figure, but from the time of the sculptor Praxiteles, who began to show the female figure nude (before that, only male figures were shown unclothed), then Aphrodite became the model for the divine beauty of the human female form, which no people since the Greeks have evoked so gloriously.

The worship of Aphrodite was generally austere, but prostitutes regarded her as their protector, and in Corinth, among other places, it appears the priestesses were also prostitutes (not by any means a unique occurrence in early, uninhibited religious cults). Aphrodite was frequently associated with certain lesser divinities, of whom the best-known is Eros (they are better known as Venus and Cupid), who was sometimes described as her son, sometimes merely as an attendant. This association is a late one; Eros does not appear in the older myths. In Homer he is *eros*, the irresistible attraction between two people: but as a personification he is as old as Earth herself, according to Hesiod. It was only in late Hellenic times that he became a rather ridiculous, chubby little boy with his darts of romantic love.

Aphrodite was sometimes also associated with the Horae, i.e. the seasons, and the Charites, rather vague personifications of virtuous qualities. But her surnames included 'the Black One' and 'Killer of

Men', and she was occasionally numbered among the Furies. Her bird is the dove, commonly supposed to be peculiarly amorous.

The most famous myth of Aphrodite concerns her relations with the beautiful Adonis, whose name means 'lord' in Near Eastern languages.

A certain king, variously identified, had a daughter Myrrha who offended Aphrodite by claiming to be more beautiful. As punishment the goddess made her fall in love with her father, and one night when he was drunk she climbed into bed with him. When her father discovered what had happened, and that his daughter was pregnant by him, he grew very angry and chased her from the house with a sword in his hand. He would have killed her, but Aphrodite intervened and at the vital moment turned Myrrha into a myrrh tree. (Myrrh was believed to be an aphrodisiac, incidentally). The father's sword cleft the bark of the tree, and from it was born Adonis.

Aphrodite gave the beautiful baby to Persephone for safe-keeping and Persephone put him into a chest in the House of Hades. Opening the chest to have a look at him one day, she was struck by his great beauty, and when Aphrodite wanted him back she was unwilling to give him up. Zeus was asked to mediate, but he found the spectacle of two goddesses quarrelling over possession of an exquisite youth, for reasons that were clearly not maternal, thoroughly unedifying, and he referred the matter to a lower tribunal, one of the Muses. In a reasonable judgment, fair to all parties – not least Adonis – she decided that he should spend one-third of the year with Aphrodite, one-third with Persephone, and one-third free of them both. Aphrodite did not stick to the letter of the agreement, for she employed her magic girdle, which made everyone fall in love with her, to retain Adonis during his free period.

The Theseum at Athens, older than the Parthenon and the best preserved of Doric temples – thanks largely to its later existence as a Christian church. In spite of its name it had nothing to do with Theseus, but was originally a temple of Hephaestus.

A votive statue, now in the museum at Reggio, of Aphrodite with Eros, here represented as her son.

Above, right:
Aphrodite with her lover, Ares, attended by Eros. From a Pompeian mural.

Annoyed, Persephone went to Ares and told him that his paramour was obsessed by an effeminate youth—and a mortal at that. The jealous war god adopted the form of a wild boar and, when Adonis went hunting, gored him to death. Anemones sprang from the ground where his blood was spilt. In other versions, the boar is identified with Apollo or Artemis rather than Ares.

Some say that Aphrodite prevailed on Zeus to release Adonis from the Underworld, where Persephone had him to herself, for half the year.

The girdle of Aphrodite was a powerful weapon and caused trouble for many, both gods and men. Even Zeus, in the *Iliad*, failed to withstand it (though not in all sources). It is said that Zeus' annoyance at the flaunting of Aphrodite led him to make her fall in love with the herdsman-king, Anchises, whom she seduced while disguised as a mortal. Anchises was understandably worried when he discovered that he had been sleeping with a goddess, but Aphrodite told him that he need not worry as long as he kept his mouth shut. (She also prophesied that they would have a famous son; this proved to be Aeneas).

Some time later, while Anchises was drinking with his friends, someone asked him if he would not rather sleep with a certain girl than with Aphrodite herself. Anchises was unable to resist the temptation to answer, truly, that the question was irrelevant as he had slept with both. Zeus overheard, and angrily threw a thunderbolt which struck down Anchises. The effect, however, was not mortal, or not permanently so, as Anchises had to reappear in order to be carried away from Troy by Aeneas. Some say Aphrodite diverted the thunderbolt with her girdle, so that it missed Anchises, others that Anchises was punished for looking on the goddess naked by being blinded by bees.

Another of Aphrodite's offspring, by either Hermes or Dionysus, was Priapus, he of the gigantic genitals, so afflicted, it is said, by Hera, who disapproved of Aphrodite's goings-on on Olympus. Priapus' origin was the Near East, where he was a significant fertility god of a type found in many early religions.

Aphrodite's lover, Ares, often seems superfluous among the Olympians. The Greeks were not a particularly warlike people; they did not, at any rate, elevate war into a kind of religion, although many of their heroes were war heroes. Moreover, there were plenty of gods present who, one would think, were capable of looking after the military side of life. Athena, surely, in her shining armour, could have performed that duty, and several other deities were associated in various ways with war. And then, Ares does not appear as a particularly effective war god, certainly not compared with his Roman counterpart, Mars. Athena had the better of him more than once, and Heracles sent him flying back to Olympus for safety.

Below, left:
Hermes Psychopompos, the conductor of souls, whose job it was to deliver the dead to Hades, with Orpheus and Eurydice. Attic relief now in Naples.

Below:
A striking bronze figure of Hermes from Sparta. The god wears his winged sandals but appears in his aspect as the herdsmen's god.

A light-hearted work, commissioned by a Syrian merchant in Delos, of Aphrodite, assisted by Eros, rejecting the advances of Pan, whom she gaily threatens with her slipper.

With the possible exception of Hephaestus, Ares is the only one of the twelve Olympian deities who was a legitimate son of Zeus and Hera. He is not popular among the gods, and Aphrodite's passion for him seems to have been wholly physical. He is associated with the country of Thrace, where people were more warlike than they were in Attica. As a war god, Ares liked battle for its own sake; he did not take sides, or if he did, he could not be relied on to stay loyal if he saw better prospects of slaughter and destruction by changing his allegiance.

There are few myths in which Ares appears as a leading character. His embarrassing exposure by Hephaestus as an adulterer is the best known. He was the father of many children, some by Aphrodite, some by other partners, including the semi-divine heroine of Athens, Aglauros. The offspring of this union was a daughter, Alcippe, who, according to Ares, was assaulted by Halirrhothius, son of Poseidon, whom Ares killed. Ares was charged with murder by the other gods, but as there were no prosecution witnesses to deny the truth of his story, he was acquitted. The hill in Athens on which the trial was held was known thereafter as the Areopagus (Hill of Ares).

Hermes is the younger-brother figure among the gods. He runs errands for them, represents no great moral principle, and is a bit of a scamp. He seems to have originated in Arcadia, and was sometimes worshipped in the form of a stone phallus; herms, square-sided pillars surmounted by a head, are named after him. Hermes is a patron of herds, of music, and of commerce, among other things. He is usually portrayed as a slim but masculine youth, a kind of junior Apollo. His great interest in the activities of men made him particularly attractive. Although he is the messenger of death, he is not grim, but amiable, and his jokes are less dire in their effect than the jokes of many of his fellow-Olympians.

Like other gods, he grew up fast. On the day of his birth, to Maia, a daughter of Atlas, by Zeus, he stole Apollo's cattle, making shoes out of grass for their feet so that they could not be tracked. Having slaughtered a couple, and hidden the rest safely, he retired to his cradle.

Apollo searched unavailingly for his missing cattle, and got Silenus and the satyrs to help him. Eventually they arrived at Maia's cave, but she scoffed at the idea that her innocent babe would have rustled fifty of Apollo's cattle. Unfortunately, the hides of the slaughtered beasts provided convincing evidence that he had, and Apollo laid the whole case before Zeus. Hermes confessed, and promised to return the missing beasts, remarking that he had only killed the two to sacrifice to the twelve gods. '*Twelve* gods?' said Apollo, 'Who is the twelfth?' Hermes politely indicated himself.

Accompanying Apollo to retrieve the cattle, Hermes produced a lyre that he had made out of the shell of a tortoise. It played so sweetly that Apollo offered to let him keep the cattle in exchange for the lyre. Hermes further ingratiated himself by making a pipe out of reeds, which he exchanged for Apollo's golden staff and some hints on how he might learn the gift of prophecy.

Hermes had a great number of love affairs, mostly with mortals, but he did once combine with Aphrodite to produce Hermaphroditus. Some say this creature was born bisexual, others say he developed his female features after a nymph who was in love with him had prayed to be united with him, her prayer being answered in what might have been considered by both parties a rather too literal manner. Hermaphrodites are not rare in mythology; several examples occur in Eastern religions.

Hermes was the god of rogues, but Dionysus' followers were altogether more dangerous. Originally, Dionysus was probably a fertility god in Thrace and Macedonia, the centre of an orgiastic cult involving human sacrifice and animal worship. Eventually, he became the god of wine, though before that it may have been beer that his followers drank. Dionysus is a riotous figure, usually accompanied by an unruly train of satyrs and maenads ('mad women'). Dionysian myths are largely concerned with people being driven mad and/or torn to pieces. They may reflect facts fairly accurately. Certainly, Dionysus' crusade to spread his worship around the world, and his destruction of opponents, must represent the growing popularity of the wine cult and conservative opposition to it.

Dionysus was a son of Zeus and of Semele, a mortal (though also identified with a non-Greek earth goddess). His childhood was as

Below, left:
Hermes gives Dionysus, whose disrupted childhood could be held to account for the turbulence of his later character, to the nymphs of Nysa, who reared him. One of the nymphs carries the thyrsus.

Below:
Dionysus, identified by his laurel wreath, thyrsus (a staff culminating in a decorative pine cone) and his drinking horn.

Bottom:
Worshippers of Dionysus, who is represented in this Roman relief as a bull.

Opposite, top :
The Acropolis from the north-west, with the temple of Nike at the right, seen from the Areopagus. This was the hill of Ares, where the god was tried, and acquitted, by his fellow gods for killing a man who violated his daughter Alcippe. Trials for homicide and intended homicide always took place there.

Bottom :
The theatre of Dionysus at Athens, seen from the Acropolis. The great dramatic festivals of ancient Greece were in honour of the god, and tragedy had its origin in his cult. The theatre was built about 330 B.C.

Left :
The statue of Hermes, carrying the young Dionysus, by the most renowned of all classical sculptors, Praxiteles. It comes from the temple of Hera at Olympia and is now in the Olympia Museum.

violent as his later career, owing to the hostility of Hera. He was torn to pieces or, alternatively, burned in the body of his mother, but reborn from Zeus' thigh. For a time he was looked after by Ino, sister of Semele, but she was driven mad by Hera and, after more violence and horror, Dionysus passed into the hands of protective nymphs who brought him up without further disasters.

Dionysus then embarked on his efforts to establish his worship, overcoming a number of opponents in the process. One well-known story appears in a play by Euripides, *Bacchae*. After various violent victories, Dionysus came to Thebes, where he was opposed by King Pentheus, who put him in prison. But Dionysus persuaded Pentheus that he should go and spy on the Maenads, conducting their wild celebrations with the women of Thebes on a nearby mountainside. He did so, was spotted, and torn to pieces by the wild women. His own mother tore off his head without realising what she was doing.

73

A striking mask of Dionysus, the god who might well be feared but could never be denied. Porphyry, in the Rhodes Museum.

Above, right
Hebe, cup-bearer to the gods. Hebe is a minor goddess who seldom figures in myth or in art. According to Hesiod, she was the daughter of Zeus and Hera. She was the goddess of blossoming youth.

At another place, three sisters resisted the Dionysian revels, in spite of the god's blandishments, delivered in the guise of a girl. He drove them mad, in which state they sacrificed the son of one of them and ate him. Subsequently they were turned into bats.

On his way to Naxos, Dionysus was captured by pirates, who planned to sell him into slavery. The ropes they had bound him with fell off, and the pilot warned his fellows that they had a god on board. They did not believe it, or did not care, so Dionysus raised a vine from the deck which entwined the mast and rigging. He turned the oars into serpents and changed himself into a lion, summoning up apparitions of wild beasts (a favourite trick of his). The pirates jumped overboard, in terror or madness, though Dionysus saved the pilot. In the sea, they all turned into dolphins, which since then have been friendly towards human beings.

Arriving at Naxos after this adventure, Dionysus discovered Ariadne, who had been abandoned by Theseus, and had several children by her. By this time he had established his worship throughout the world, having travelled as far as India (a late story, obviously) and Africa. So he went to Mount Olympus, and was accepted by the gods as one of themselves. Some say that he took the place of Hestia, goddess of the hearth—a quiet creature hardly figuring in the myths—who resigned it willingly in the knowledge that she would be welcome in any home on earth.

The Heroes

The heroes of Greek mythology were supermen but mortals, usually having a deity as one of their parents, occasionally winning immortality in the end. They performed great deeds, often with the help of the gods, sometimes in the face of godly opposition. They are frequently the founders of cities and dynasties, and some of their exploits were no doubt manufactured to glorify the heritage of a particular city. The heroes sometimes acted alone and sometimes—as a rule later—they acted together (as in the war against Troy), a reflection of growing political co-operation. This chapter recounts some of the myths of individual heroes; the next chapter is concerned with the heroes of Thebes, which forms a separate story, and the chapter following deals chiefly with combined enterprises, plus the travels of Odysseus.

There is a great difference between an early hero, like Heracles, and a late one, like Odysseus. The latter is as vivid a character as anyone in literature; Heracles' individuality is but mistily defined. This is largely the result of literary coincidence—that Odysseus is the hero of Homer—but it is also a sign of a developing society, growing more subtle, more experienced. Heracles depends almost entirely on his brawny muscles to perform his exploits; Odysseus overcomes his problems by cunning.

Heracles may originally have been based on a real man, though his identity has been lost in the myths. Of all the great mythical heroes of Greece, he is probably the oldest. He is, however, the greatest—the hero's hero, as it were—and resembles hero-figures in other mythologies, notably the Babylonian Gilgamesh. His personal qualities, good and bad, are traditionally masculine. He is strong and brave, a lover of action, but also generous and compassionate; he has large appetites, especially for food and women, and sometimes gets into a terrific rage. He is not, however, as idiotic or as brainless as he is sometimes made to appear in his Roman version, Hercules. Though popular throughout Greece, he is most closely associated with Tiryns, a great city in Mycenean times, second only to Mycenae itself. He was also claimed by Thebes as a native of that city.

According to the Theban legend, Heracles was the son of Alcmene by Zeus, who lay with this respectable lady by taking the form of her husband. He found her so attractive that he had Hermes arrange matters so that one night lasted for three, to the annoyance of Helios who resented such an interruption to his regular schedule.

Hera was, as usual, angry with Zeus for his unfaithfulness, and what particularly annoyed her was that she knew the child of this particular union was destined for greatness. She therefore determined to make life difficult for him. First of all she managed to deny him his political inheritance. Zeus had intended that Heracles should be

the ruler of the land he was born in, but Hera had tricked him into swearing that this office would fall on the first child to be born with Zeus' blood in his veins. In the normal course of events, this would have been Heracles, but Hera delayed the birth until another child, Eurystheus, a descendant of Zeus and Danae (whom Zeus had seduced in the form of a shower of gold), was born.

The first test of the strength of the infant Heracles was not long delayed. Whether at Hera's doing or not, two snakes were placed in the cradle which Heracles shared with his twin brother, whose father was Alcmene's regular husband. The mortal child hopped out and ran for it, but Heracles merely seized the snakes and throttled them, bouncing up and down and chuckling as he did so. Another rather attractive version of this story says that the snakes were actually

Heracles and the Ceryneian hind. The 'hind' was probably a stag, if the picture is to be taken seriously, since the hero has broken off a horn. He is watched by Athena (left) and Artemis.

Opposite, top:
The infant Heracles strangling the snakes in his cradle. From a 4th-century coin.

Bottom:
Heracles and Athena, one of the carved metopes of the temple of Zeus at Olympia. Heracles is showing the goddess evidence of some Labour he has completed, perhaps the rout of the Stymphalian Birds.

quite harmless and were placed in the cradle by Alcmene's husband, who wanted to find out which of the twins was his and which the child of Zeus. The ensuing events left him in no doubt.

In Greek myth, in spite of his feats of strength, Heracles is not portrayed as a giant; one account even calls him rather short (others only six feet). In art he is a normally muscular man, not physically different from other fine male figures. It was the Romans who turned him into a kind of classical Mr Universe.

Heracles had the benefit of a good education. Castor and Pollux instructed him in warfare and duelling, a particularly fierce son of Apollo gave him boxing lessons, and some say that Apollo himself taught him archery. He also, it is said, received lessons in literature, astronomy, philosophy and music from various distinguished experts, though one cannot help thinking that such subjects were of peripheral value to Heracles. However, he was no fool. When charged with murder, after he had killed one of his music-teachers, he was able to plead – successfully – that he had been merely resisting aggression, a sufficient defence according to a law of Rhadamanthys.

His step-father felt that it would nevertheless be advisable for the young Heracles to be removed from circulation for a time, and sent him off to look after the cattle in a distant pasture until he was eighteen. There he fought with and killed a lion which was preying on the cattle. His weapon was a club made from an untrimmed olive tree. One of the cattle owners, King Thespius, gave him lodging during the lion hunt, which involved sleeping with every one of his host's fifty daughters.

Heracles' most famous exploits, the Twelve Labours, were performed as a condition for his release from the service of Eurystheus (King of Tiryns due to his earlier birth). There are several variants of the story of how he came to be placed in Eurystheus' service, but the commonest one is that it was a punishment for Heracles' murder of his wife Megara, daughter of the King of Thebes, who gave her to him after Heracles had fought successfully against invaders of the city. Hera is held responsible for this fearful crime: she afflicted Heracles with madness so that he thought Megara and their children were enemies, and slaughtered all of them. But some say this happened *after* the Twelve Labours. (The legends of Heracles come from many sources, some are inevitably contradictory, and any kind of coherent chronology is virtually impossible).

The exploits of Heracles were a popular subject in Greek art, and this black-figured Athenian cup shows the hero wrestling with Nereus, the sea god. Note the frieze of Nereids.

Opposite:
The Cyclopean walls of Tiryns are over twenty feet thick, with vaulted passages where food was stored during a siege. Traditionally, Tiryns was the city of Heracles, and one may think that someone of his physical capacity would be handy in erecting these massive frotifications. The illustration shows a sally port in the north wall.

It was on the advice of the priestess of Delphi that Heracles went to Tiryns and put himself at the service of Eurystheus. He did so reluctantly, knowing himself to be a better man than the king, and the promise of immortality at the end of his Labours failed to lighten his spirits.

The First Labour was the killing of the Nemean Lion. This formidable beast could not be harmed by weapons of stone or metal. It lived in a cave near the city of Nemea, and had been introduced to the spot by an angry goddess, some say Hera, and had depopulated the place. Finding his arrows and sword made no impression, Heracles struck the lion a mighty blow with his club, whereat it appeared dazed. He closed with it and, after it had bitten off one of his fingers, choked it to death. Then he skinned it with its own claws and from that day forward wore its pelt over his shoulders. He wore no other clothing, nor did he, as a rule bother with the weapons that Athena (always an admirer of Heracles) and Hephaestus had given him. He relied on his olive-tree club and his bow.

A relief from the 6th-century temple of Assos, showing Heracles putting the Centaurs to flight during the battle in which he inadvertently gave Chiron his incurable wound.

Eurystheus was alarmed by Heracles' return, wearing the Nemean Lion's skin, and he had a large bronze urn made; on future occasions when Heracles reappeared with some horrid monster, Eurystheus would jump into the pot for safety.

The object of the Second Labour was another fearful monster, the Hydra, which had a body like a huge dog and at least nine snake-like heads, one of which was immortal. In this Labour, Heracles was assisted, as usual, by Athena, and also by Iolaus, his nephew and faithful squire. He found the Hydra a very formidable proposition. As fast as he bashed in its heads, more appeared; a huge crab joined in as an ally of the Hydra, but Heracles crushed it with his foot (his arms being fully occupied wrestling with the Hydra). The problem of the multiplying heads was overcome by Iolaus thrusting a burning brand at each severed neck, which prevented new heads growing. The immortal head Heracles cut off and buried, still hissing angrily. Then he dipped his arrows in the dead monster's blood, which made them deadly ever after.

A subsidiary problem of Heracles' labours was that some of the creatures he was ordered to subdue had special connections with some god or goddess. This was the case with the Ceryneian hind. Originally there were five of these very large, bronze-hoofed hinds (or stags), but the other four had been harnessed by Artemis to her chariot. Heracles did not seek to kill the Ceryneian hind, but hunted it for half a year, until it was exhausted and he captured it. Even so, Artemis was not pleased by this treatment of her favourite, and demanded an explanation. Heracles replied that he was merely obeying orders, and Artemis let the matter drop. Robert Graves has ingeniously suggested that the hind was a reindeer, as only reindeer does have antlers (admittedly, not gold ones, like those of the Ceryneian hind) and only reindeers can be successfully employed as harness animals. They are also larger than any species known to the Greeks. It is possible that the Greeks had heard tell of reindeer, although the nearest ones are, of course, a very long way from Greece.

On Mount Erymanthus lived a fierce wild boar, which ravaged the country round about. The Fourth Labour of Heracles was to capture this beast. On his way he was entertained by the Centaur, Pholus, who gave him meat but was reluctant to broach the Centaurs' communal wine jar. Heracles insisted, and the other Centaurs, attracted by the smell of the wine, attacked. The hero repelled them, in spite of a rain storm which slackened the string of his bow, but two most unfortunate accidents occurred during the mêlée. Chiron, the wise Centaur, came to see what the noise was about, and a stray arrow from Heracles' bow wounded him in the knee. Because of the Hydra's poison, it would not heal; the despairing Chiron eventually passed his immortality to Prometheus and embraced death, which alone would relieve him of his pain. Then Pholus, who was puzzled by the deadly effect of Heracles' arrows, picked one up to look at it. Clumsily he dropped it, it pierced his foot, and he died at once.

After the disastrous fight with the Centaurs, capturing the Erymanthian boar must have been almost like a holiday. He skilfully drove it uphill into the snows, which slowed it down so that he could seize it and bind it with chains. He carried it back to Argos, where Eurystheus took one look at it and jumped into his bronze pot. Some say that it was on his return from this Labour that Heracles found the Argonauts about to sail in search of the Golden Fleece, and disobediently joined them. He is, however, a minor character in that legend.

Below, left :
Heracles driving off the Stymphalian Birds, apparently with a sling. From a 5th-century amphora in the British Museum.

Right :
The Cretan bull succumbs to Heracles. From the metopes of the temple of Zeus at Olympia, 5th century. Many of these sadly damaged relics are now in the Louvre.

Bottom :
Heracles, having killed Geryon and the dog, Orthrus, prepares to drive off Geryon's cattle.

81

The Stymphalian birds, the object of Heracles' Fifth Labour, were sacred to Ares. Various versions of why they had to be extinguished exist, but the most authentic explains that they were razor-winged man-eaters. They lived in the Stymphalian Marsh, near Mount Cyllene, and at first Heracles could think of no way of getting at them. He could not walk in the soft mud, and he could not move a boat through the dense reeds. Athena proposed a workable plan, and on her advice he took a bronze rattle up a mountain and made such a tremendous din that the startled birds flew up from the marsh and Heracles shot them down. He repeated this trick several times, and the rest of the flock flew away to the east, settling on the Isle of Ares in the Black Sea.

The Sixth Labour of Heracles was to clean out the stables of King Augeias at Elis. Eurystheus, jealous of Heracles, was especially

Heracles returns from the Underworld with Cerberus on a leash, and a horrified Eurystheus ducks into his home-made shelter, a huge storage jar.

pleased with this idea, as the Augeian stables were piled high with dung accumulated over many years. Nevertheless, Heracles accomplished the task in a single day, by diverting the course of the river Alphaeus to run through the stables.

After his Sixth Labour, Heracles was sent farther afield by Eurystheus; perhaps there were no monsters left for him to tackle in the Peloponnese.

For his Seventh Labour, he sailed to Crete to tackle the Cretan bull, a fire-breathing animal that was trampling the crops in that island. Some suggest that it was the bull which had brought Europa to Crete. King Minos was anxious to help, but Heracles pursued the bull alone. He captured it and brought it back to show Eurystheus, who set it free.

Next he went to Thrace, where four savage mares were terrorizing the countryside. These man-eating horses were the property of King Diomedes, a son of Ares, and, after capturing the mares, Heracles had to deal with the king and his followers. He rid himself of the pursuing army by cutting a channel for the sea which flooded the plain, and having struck Diomedes with his club, fed him to his own mares. This tamed them, and Heracles carried them off.

Heracles' Ninth Labour also required him to fight the children of Ares. These were the Amazons, warrior-women who lived near the Black Sea. Heracles was charged with obtaining the girdle of their queen, Hippolyte, given to her by Ares as a sign of her superiority over other women. It was desired by Admete, daughter of Eurystheus. On the way to and from the country of the Amazons, Heracles had numerous adventures. He took part in several wars, one boxing match and two wrestling bouts; on each occasion he was victorious. He was also successful in obtaining Hippolyte's girdle, though there are many versions of how this was done.

Heracles' Tenth Labour was to steal the cattle of Geryon from their owner. Geryon was a man-monster who divided into three at the waist, having six arms and three heads. He was the strongest man alive, and lived far in the west with his gorgeous red cattle, guarded by their herdsman Eurytion (another son of Ares) and a two-headed watchdog, Orthrus. (Creatures, and indeed gods, with multiple limbs are a feature of many mythologies, notably in India).

Above, left:
Atlas shows Heracles the Apples of the Hesperides, which he has obtained while the hero, with a helping hand from Athena, fills in as supporter of the heavens. Another superb fragment from the metopes of the temple of Zeus at Olympia.

Above:
Leaning on his club, Heracles is seen in a rare moment of relaxation in the garden of the Hesperides.

Theseus sails away from Naxos –
and abandons Ariadne, the
king's daughter who had helped
him defeat the Minotaur. Fresco
painting from Pompeii.

Below :
Hippolytus spurns the love of
Phaedra, his stepmother. A
Roman mosaic of the 3rd century
A.D. from Paphos.

On his way west, Heracles again took part in many wars. At the western end of the Mediterranean he erected two pillars on either side of the straits of Gibraltar. The sun was too hot, so he fired an arrow at it, but when Helios protested he at once packed up his bow and apologised. Helios was so charmed by this unexpectedly amenable reaction, that he gave Heracles a huge golden goblet as a boat in which to continue his journey. Arriving at his destination, he despatched first Orthrus and then Eurytion with his club, and drove off the cattle. Geryon challenged him to battle and Heracles, moving round his flank, fired an arrow that pierced all three bodies of Geryon, killing him. Hera, attempting to aid Geryon, also received an arrow from the intrepid hero's bow, and fled the scene. On his way home, Heracles performed many deeds of valour, founded cities and begot sons who became the founders of new races, such as the Scythians. At one point, he arrived in Sicily, having turned right too soon after crossing the Alps and travelling the length of Italy before he realised his mistake. (Needless to say, this is a Roman interpolation, found in Ovid and other Latin writers).

At some stage in their careers, most heroes had to confront the Underworld, and the Eleventh Labour of Heracles was nothing less than the abduction of Cerberus, the frightful, black, multi-headed hound that guards the gates of hell. This was the hardest of his tasks (perhaps it ought to come last) and was only accomplished with the aid of friendly gods. No doubt it represents Heracles' successful challenge to mortality.

On his way through the Underworld, guided by Hermes, Heracles had many interesting encounters. One story says he fought with Hades himself. He met Meleager among the ghosts and offered to marry his sister, Deianira. He found his friend Theseus, stuck to a chair, and wrenched him free. (Stories about Theseus frequently become intermingled with those about Heracles). He frightened Charon into ferrying him across the Styx, and at last confronted Cerberus. Hades told him he could take the hound of hell if he could overcome him without weapons. Heracles seized Cerberus by the throat; the hound's barbed serpent-tail reared up but was deflected by Heracles' lion-skin cape, and at length Cerberus was forced to submit. With Athena's help, he got back across the Styx and dragged Cerberus through dark passages and up to the light of the sun.

Many stories are attached to the myth of Heracles and Cerberus. It is said, for example, that aconites first grew from the saliva that Cerberus spat on the fields.

The Twelfth and last Labour had a much less formidable objective, though not an easy one: the Golden Apples of the Hesperides. The tree which bore these desirable fruits had been a wedding present to Hera from Mother Earth. It was guarded by a dragon and grew in the west, on the slopes of Mount Atlas. The Hesperides, daughters of Atlas, were wont to pilfer the apples; hence the dragon. Heracles forced the sea-god, Nereus, to show him how to get the apples. (Nereus, father of the Nereids, was once an important figure, but he tended to become merged with the more popular Poseidon). On reaching his destination, Heracles killed the dragon with an arrow; alternatively, he asked Atlas to get the apples for him, volunteering to take over the job of holding up the heavens while he did so. Atlas soon returned with three apples, but suggested that, if Heracles would kindly stay where he was for a short time, he would take the apples to Eurystheus himself. Heracles had been warned by Nereus that Atlas might make some excuse to avoid holding up heaven any longer, but, for once using brain rather than brawn, he replied that

Amazons, on an Ionian silver relief of the 6th century B.C. It is not known why the idea of a race of warrior maidens should have been so interesting to the Greeks but they appear frequently in the stories of the heroes. A later tradition made Ares and Artemis their patron deities: but the Amazons were described as the daughters of Ares in older stories.

Heracles and his captives, the Cercopes, who in spite of their predicament are grinning over their vulgar jokes at the hero's expense.

Right:
In this Roman mural from Pompeii (1st century A.D.), a bronzed Heracles watches as his son, Telephus, is suckled by a hind. The intense-looking female figure is a personification of Arcadia.

Below:
Heracles feared no one, not even the god Apollo. This scene on an Attic amphora portrays a famous incident at Delphi, when the two struggled for possession of the sacred tripod. Zeus had to separate them with a strategically hurled thunderbolt.

he was quite agreeable but would Atlas just take over for a moment as he wished to put a hat on? Easily fooled, Atlas did so. Heracles picked up the apples and left.

It is sometimes said that Heracles' original task was to perform Ten Labours only. An extra two were added because Eurystheus would not accept that two had been properly performed: against the Hydra Heracles had been helped by Iolaus, and the job of cleaning the Augeian Stables had not been completed by him but by the river.

Dozens of stories are told of the feats of Heracles, during his Twelve Labours or at other times. There is a certain monotony about some of them, but others have striking individual touches and one or two, like the story of the Cercopes, are comic.

The Cercopes were a couple of plausible rogues, expert thieves, and monkey-like in appearance (they ended up as total monkeys, a punishment for playing tricks on the gods). Heracles caught them trying to steal his weapons, tied their legs to a pole which he swung across his shoulder and carried them off to justice. In that position the Cercopes had, perforce, a close-up view of the hero's private parts: he was wearing no clothes, as usual. After a while the Cercopes started chuckling between themselves. It turned out that their mother had warned them to beware of 'the man with the black backside'. As Heracles' upper body was protected by his lion-skin cape, his backside was more sunburnt than the rest of him, and now the Cercopes knew what their mother had been talking about. Their further humorous exchanges about Heracles' nether regions finally started him laughing too, and he was persuaded to let them go.

Heracles' second wife was Deianira, as he had promised Meleager's ghost. (Deianira's father, however, was the god Dionysus). He won her after a fight with a rival suitor, Achelous, a river-god, whose ability to change suddenly into a serpent or a bull did not avail him much against the strength of Heracles. After defeating Achelous,

A small, very early (8th century) bronze of a man and a centaur, perhaps embracing, more likely fighting. It is interesting that at this time the centaur was portrayed as a complete man, with part of a horse added. The height of the figure is about 4½ inches.

Right:
Another of Heracles' conquests. Achelous, who adopted a serpentine form as a temporary expedient, was his rival for the hand of Deianira. Heracles is about to break off Achelous' horn.

Below:
Heracles with his wife, Deianira, and their son. From a red-figure vase in the Fitzwilliam Museum, Cambridge.

Below, right:
Heracles, Deianira and the Centaur Nessus – an encounter that led indirectly to Heracles' death. A Roman mural from Pompeii.

Heracles carried Deianira off. On their journey they came to a flooded river, where the Centaur Nessus volunteered to carry Deianira over on his back. But no sooner was she mounted than the Centaur ran off with her, and was about to rape her when Heracles shot him with an arrow from a range of half a mile. As Nessus lay dying, he advised Deianira to take some of his blood and, if Heracles ever showed signs of being unfaithful, to smear it on his clothes as it would keep him faithful.

Thereafter, Heracles did have many lovers, but it was not until he fell in love with Iole, who had been kept from him after he had won her fairly in an archery contest, causing him to kill her entire family, that Deianira decided to try the charm of Nessus. Of course, Nessus had been dissembling. Since he had been shot by one of Heracles' poisonous arrows, he knew his blood would be poisonous too. When Heracles put on the anointed shirt, the poison began to work, burning his flesh away from the bones. Deianira killed herself in horror at her mistake, and the prophecy of Zeus was fulfilled, that no living creature should kill Heracles; he would die at the hands of an enemy already dead.

Heracles ordered the construction of his own funeral pyre, spread his lion-skin cape upon it, and lay down to die. There was some difficulty in finding a volunteer to light the fire, but at last a passing shepherd agreed to do so. Heracles gave him his bow and arrows in gratitude. No sooner was the fire lit than Zeus hurled a thunderbolt which reduced the pyre to ashes. The mortal body of Heracles was dead. But the immortal part lived on, and Zeus received him on Olympus as a god, remarking that any deity who did not like the idea would have to put up with it. Hera swallowed her annoyance and said nothing. Subsequently, at Zeus' order, Heracles underwent a symbolic form of rebirth as the son of Hera, and from that time on Hera loved him next only to Zeus himself. Heracles became the gate-keeper of heaven, and often used to admit Artemis in the evening after she had been hunting. He would look at her bag of hares and wild goats and shake his head, advising her to hunt ravaging boars, mad bulls, lions and wolves, as more sporting prey.

While Heracles was an immensely popular mythological figure in Greece and beyond, he was not generally regarded as a true god, and was not an Olympian in the Greek pantheon. However, there were a few cults associated with him in various places.

Theseus—some of whose exploits seem to have been taken over by Heracles, or vice-versa—was an Athenian hero, the founder of that city's greatness. His father was either Aegeus, an early king of Athens, or as some say, Poseidon, the brother of Zeus who ruled the waters—and certainly gave valuable assistance to Theseus at many decisive moments. (In view of the obvious connection between the

Theseus carrying off Hippolyte (or Antiope), the Amazon queen. Some say he killed her, and the legend seems to be confused with an exploit of Heracles.

Above, left:
Theseus subduing the much-travelled bull which Heracles had captured and brought from Crete. From an Attic red-figured vase.

The death of the Minotaur, on a black-figure amphora. The attendant figures, which usefully fill up the space, are presumably the young Athenians intended for sacrifice to the monster.

Above, right:
Theseus taking part in the battle of the Lapiths against the Centaurs, one of whom, having seized Laodameia, he is about to strike.

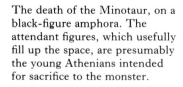

names of Aegeus and the Aegean Sea, perhaps Aegeus and Poseidon were originally one and the same). When Aegeus was returning to Athens from Delphi, it is said, he stopped at Troezen and made love to a princess, Aethra. Before continuing his journey home, he left his sword and sandals concealed under a heavy rock. He told Aethra that any son of hers who could lift the rock and recover his possessions he would acknowledge as his heir. In due course Theseus was born to Aethra, and when he had reached the age of sixteen, no doubt a strapping youth, his mother brought him to the rock, which he raised without undue difficulty, revealing the sword and sandals of Aegeus. He had only to travel to Athens to be acknowledged as its future king.

Theseus scorned the easy route to Athens by sea, preferring instead to take the more dangerous overland route. On the way he encountered, and overcame, a succession of more or less monstrous creatures, in a saga similar to the Twelve Labours of Heracles. Most of these creatures seem to have had attractive daughters on whom, again resembling Heracles, Theseus fathered children.

The first of the mythological highwaymen that Theseus met was Periphetes the Club-man, who used to bludgeon all passers-by. Theseus seized his club, which he kept ever after, and killed Periphetes with it. On the Isthmus of the Peloponnese lived Sirius, whose practice it was to tie his victims to the tops of two pine trees, bent down to the ground. He then let the trees go, and the victims were torn apart. Theseus killed him in the same manner. At Crommyum he hunted the Grey Sow, which had driven the people from their fields, and killed it. Following the cliff road along the coast, Theseus met his next opponent, Sciron, who would compel travellers to wash his feet and, as they crouched to do so, would kick them over the cliffs to a man-eating turtle waiting below. Theseus refused to wash Sciron's feet, and hurled the hideous practical joker to the turtle. At Eleusis there was an amazingly powerful wrestler, Cercyon, who crushed opponents to death by his mighty strength. But Theseus knew—had, indeed, invented—the art of wrestling, and threw Cercyon, who struck his head on the ground and was killed. Near Athens, Theseus conquered the sixth and last of his opponents, another creature with a nasty sense of humour, Procrustes. For Procrustes had a bed, on which he insisted that all wayfarers should lie. But they had to fit the bed exactly. If they did not, Procrustes would either stretch them or chop parts off, for neatness' sake.

Perseus escaping from the sisters of Medusa, whose head he has cut off and is holding, on Pegasus. In a better-known version of the myth, Perseus was able to fly himself, thanks to Hermes, and did not need a flying horse. From the decapitated body of the Gorgon emerges Chrysaor, who was to be the father of the monster (and successful rancher) Geryon. This terra-cotta relief comes from Melos and is now in the British Museum.

Below :
In this companion piece Pegasus is ridden by Bellerophon, who is about to slay the Chimaera.

The exploits of Theseus at a glance: in the centre, his killing of the Minotaur; around the circumference, wrestling with Cercyon, trimming Procrustes to size, despatching Sinis, capturing the bull of Marathon, throwing Sciron off the cliff, and hunting the monstrous sow.

Theseus fitted the bed, however, then he made Procrustes lie down on it. Unfortunately for Procrustes, he did not fit.

Finally, Theseus arrived in Athens. But his welcome was not universally warm. Aegeus had married Medea, the witch-queen brought back by Jason, and had a son by her. The jealous Medea suggested to Aegeus that the newcomer was a pretender. She offered Theseus a poisoned cup, but just in time Aegeus recognised the sword that Theseus was wearing as his own, and knocked the cup away as his son was about to drink.

Medea departed under a cloud, and there was great rejoicing in Athens. Theseus took the lead in the battle against Pallas and his sons, who had rebelled against Aegeus, then he captured and caught the Marathonian bull (the same bull that Heracles had brought back from Crete), which he sacrificed to Apollo. Next, Theseus himself sailed to Crete, on what is his most famous exploit, to kill the Minotaur.

Returning from Naxos, where he had abandoned Ariadne to Dionysus, Theseus forgot to change his sails from black to white, with the result that Aegeus presumed him dead and jumped into the sea named after him, leaving the kingdom vacant for Theseus. (This story may reflect an ancient rite in which a king was actually thrown from a rock to make way for his successor).

As king of Athens, Theseus was credited with forming the union of Attic settlements as a federalized, Athenian state. (This union certainly took place and was probably effected by a great statesman; here, myth seems to approach history very closely). He had to resist rebellions and an invasion by the Amazons, whose queen, Hippolyta, he married. It is not clear whether this Hippolyta was the same as the lady whose girdle Heracles was charged with obtaining; probably the myths of Heracles and Theseus have become confused.

Theseus married again after the death of Hippolyta, but his second wife, Phaedra, fell in love with her stepson, Hippolytus, son of Hippolyta. While Theseus was away, she made advances to him, but he rejected her and Phaedra hanged herself, leaving behind a letter which accused Hippolytus of having seduced her. Theseus, reading the letter, pronounced a curse upon his son, a curse which Poseidon had guaranteed would be effective. Later, Theseus discovered his mistake, but by that time it was too late, for Hippolytus, driving along the coast road, had encountered a sea monster which frightened his horses, overturning the carriage and killing the unfortunate driver.

Theseus took part in a number of other adventures, some of which sound as if they had been invented to create a parallel with the Twelve Labours of Heracles; none of them, certainly, compare with his destruction of the Minotaur. His last exploits took place in co-operation with Pirithous, King of the Lapiths, whose battles with the Centaurs (symbolizing the victory of Athenian civilization over barbarism) were so brilliantly depicted in the sculptures of the Parthenon. With Pirithous, Theseus descended to Hades in an attempt to abduct Persephone, whom Pirithous wished to have as a wife. It was on that journey that Theseus was imprisoned in a chair, from which he could not move until Heracles pulled him free.

Back in Athens, Theseus found a usurper on the throne, and was forced into exile. He fled to the island of Scyros, where he died – according to some accounts, thrown off a cliff by the King of Scyros.

In Argos lived a king called Acrisius, who had no son to supplant him but a daughter, Danae, whom he kept locked up because he had been warned by an oracle that if she produced a son, that son would kill him. But Danae had already attracted the eye of Zeus, who visited her in her locked chamber in the form of a shower of gold. The fruit of their union was a son, Perseus, 'the Destroyer'.

When Danae gave birth to the dreaded grandson, Acrisius set them both adrift in the sea in an ark. The ark floated to the island of Seriphos, where a fisherman brought it ashore. The King of Seriphos, Polydectes, took the abandoned pair into his own house; he fell in love with Danae who, however, rejected him – a tense situation. Perseus, having grown up with the customary speed of mythological heroes, naturally supported his mother, and when Polydectes announced that he intended to marry another lady, Perseus declared that he would willingly obtain for him any gift he liked as part of the bride-price. He would even get him the Gorgon's Head. Polydectes leapt on this rash promise. The Gorgon's Head would indeed be a most acceptable gift, he said, thinking that such a quest would remove Perseus permanently.

The Gorgon's Head belonged to Medusa (though it appears to have had a separate existence at some other time: it appeared as a motif on the shield of Athena, for example, though some say Athena got it from Perseus). It was extremely ugly, having tusk-like teeth, a protruding tongue, and snakes instead of hair. Anyone who looked at it was immediately turned to stone.

All the monster-killing heroes of the Greeks relied to some extent on divine assistance. Perseus was especially fortunate in this respect. Athena presented him with a brightly polished shield; Hermes provided winged sandals, a magic bag in which to carry the head, and

In this scene in relief on the back of a mirror, Phaedra, prompted by Eros, declares her disastrous love for Hippolytus to her nurse.

A shower of gold (alias Zeus) descends upon Danae, who will give birth to Perseus as a result. Red-figure painting of the 5th century, now in Leningrad.

Left:
Danae with her infant Perseus and husband Acrisius. From a Pompeian fresco, 1st century A.D.

Perseus with the head of Medusa. This fragment of carved ivory comes from Samos and dates from the early 6th century B.C.

Below :
Pompeian painting of Bellerophon, aided by Athena, putting a bridle on the wild Pegasus.

a sickle to chop it off; Hades a helmet that made its wearer invisible. However, these latter gifts were not obtained without difficulty, as they were held by certain nymphs whose residence was unknown to Perseus. He had to find out where they lived from the Graeae, three sisters of the Gorgons. These swan-like females owned only one eye and one tooth between them, which they used to share. Perseus waited until eye and tooth were in transit, so to speak, grabbed them, and refused to give them back until the Graeae told him what he wanted to know. (Some say it was the location of the Gorgons that Perseus found out from the Graeae).

Arriving in the African desert, the land of the Gorgons, Perseus found them asleep, surrounded by the weather-worn images of petrified men. Guided by Athena, he flew (thanks to the winged sandals) up to Medusa, keeping his back turned and watching her image reflected in his shield, and cut off her head with the sickle. With eyes averted, he pushed the head into the bag he carried. Medusa's sister-Gorgons were awakened by her children, Pegasus the winged horse and Chrysaor the warrior (their father was Poseidon), but they could not catch Perseus, who had put on the helmet that made him invisible.

Flying home—assisted by Hermes at times, for the bag with the Gorgon's head in it was extremely heavy—Perseus spotted a beautiful naked girl chained to a rock on the coast. She was destined to be eaten by a sea monster, a sacrifice demanded by the Nereids because her mother had claimed to be more beautiful than they. Perseus descended, killed the monster after a fearful fight (though some say he used the Gorgon's head to turn it to stone), and released the maiden, Andromeda, from her predicament. Andromeda was the daughter of King Cepheus and the boastful Queen Cassiopeia, who could hardly refuse Perseus' request for their daughter's hand. However, there was a rival, supported by Cassiopeia, who arrived with armed retainers to claim Andromeda for himself. Out-numbered, Perseus was forced to use the devastating weapon he had acquired by his decapitation of Medusa, and turned his opponents to stone.

Perseus rescuing Andromeda from the rock, a wall painting from Pompeii. The subject has been a popular one with later artists, and this rather static, though technically accomplished painting, is possibly a copy of an earlier one.

Below :
The Chimaera, a really frightening monster, resisting the efforts of men to overcome it. Bellerophon, with the advantage of a winged horse, accomplished the task. This amphora is in the British Museum.

When he arrived in Seriphos with Andromeda, Perseus found his mother in dire straits. Determinedly resisting Polydectes, she had taken refuge in the temple where Polydectes, though he could not violate sanctuary by using force against her, was refusing her food. Perseus turned Polydectes and his entire court into stone. It is said that a circle of boulders on Seriphos marks their remains.

Leaving Polydectes' brother as king of Seriphos, Perseus with his wife and mother sailed to Argos, where he had been born. Acrisius, hearing of their approach, hurriedly departed to another country, but by an unlucky accident—or the will of the gods—Perseus was invited there to take part in some games; the discus that he threw was carried off course and struck Acrisius, killing him. Thus were the words of the oracle fulfilled. (Judging by the frequency of death by discus, the ancient Greek games were not as well organized from the safety point of view as they might have been).

As for Perseus, he became, some say, a great king and the founder of Mycenae. Another account says that, grieving at his accidental killing of Acrisius, Perseus went to Asia where his son Perses became king of the Persians, giving his name to that nation.

The story of Bellerophon is connected at several points with that of Perseus, his fellow monster-killer. Bellerophon was a hero of Corinth, said to be a son of Poseidon, whose adventures start at the court of King Proetus, brother of Acrisius, at Tiryns. He was a

Atalanta hunting on horseback.
Mosaic of the 4th century A.D.

somewhat unwelcome guest, having fled from Corinth after killing his brother, and he was soon in trouble at Tiryns also. Extremely handsome, Bellerophon was desired by Proetus' wife who, like Phaedra, revenged herself for her rejection by accusing the young man of doing exactly what he had declined to do. Proetus then sent him to Lycia, with a sealed letter to Iobates, king of Lycia, requesting Bellerophon's death. Accordingly, Iobates set the hero a number of military tasks which, like Polydectes sending Perseus in pursuit of Medusa, he expected would result in the hero's death.

Bellerophon is commonly associated with the winged horse, Pegasus, the offspring of Poseidon and Medusa (and thus, incidentally, his half-brother), which he captured with the aid of Athena. However, in the earlier version of the Bellerophon legend, Pegasus does not appear.

The first task of Bellerophon was to kill the fire-breathing Chimaera. This nightmarish creature was, from head to tail, lion, goat, and serpent. She is usually represented in Greek art as basically a lion, with tail ending in a serpent's head and the head and neck of a goat emerging from her back. The word itself means 'she-goat'; nowadays it describes a non-existent menace.

With or without the aid of Pegasus, Bellerophon destroyed the Chimaera. One description of how he did so is particularly ingenious: he stuck a lump of lead on the end of his spear and thrust it into the monster's mouth; her fiery breath melted the lead, which flowed down her throat and burnt out her guts.

Iobates next sent Bellerophon to fight two savage tribes, the Solymians and the Amazons. He overcame them both, some say by flying high above them on Pegasus and dropping rocks on their heads, and Iobates was forced to employ more direct methods. This time he sent his own Lycian soldiers to ambush Bellerophon. With the aid of Poseidon, Bellerophon defeated them also, and Iobates belatedly concluded that his intended victim enjoyed divine protection. Some say that he confronted Bellerophon with Proteus' letter, and thus heard the true facts of the affair at Tiryns. Relieved, he gave his daughter to Bellerophon in marriage, and made the Corinthian hero heir to his kingdom.

Unfortunately, the story of Bellerophon does not, after all, end happily. Later writers say that he became ambitious and tried to ride up to heaven, at which an indignant Zeus sent a fly to sting Pegasus, making him rear suddenly and throw Bellerophon to the earth. Earlier writers describe the sad deaths of his children, including his daughter, who had lain with Zeus and produced one of the Trojan heroes, Sarpedon, as a result. Whatever the cause, Bellerophon ended his days a lonely vagrant, wandering gloomily through the world and avoiding the ways of men.

Meleager, the Calydonian hero, figures briefly in a number of minor myths, and the most famous story in which he plays a part was, strictly, not an individual enterprise but a joint one, the Calydonian Boar Hunt. But as he was the leader of that enterprise, and as he is often loosely associated with heroes like Bellerophon or Perseus, while dying before the Trojan War, he fits most comfortably into this chapter.

The Aetolian dynasty to which Meleager belonged was genealogically complicated, largely owing to the frequent infusion of divine blood. Meleager's ostensible father was Oeneus, the first man to receive the vine from Dionysus. However, Oeneus' daughter Deianira (wife of Heracles) and his son Meleager are said to have been the children of Dionysus and Ares respectively.

Oeneus incurred the anger of Artemis because, when sacrificing the first fruits of his vineyard to the gods, he left her out. In pique she sent an enormous boar to ravage the land. Meleager volunteered to lead an expedition to get rid of this beast. The party included several of the Argonauts, including Jason, plus Theseus, Castor and Pollux, and several other great names, as well as a notable female hunter, Atalanta. The boar's chances, one cannot help thinking, were extremely slim from the outset.

There is no surviving account of the Calydonian Boar Hunt to compare with the Quest of the Golden Fleece, still less the Trojan War, but it is clear that this legend was more important to the Greeks than might be supposed from what we know of it.

After prolonged feasting, the expedition set off. Like all expeditions that include too many individualists in their number, it was not

The climax of the Calydonian boar hunt. Meleager is immediately right of the boar (one of whose victims lies under the beast) and the dog Leucios has sprung on to the boar's back. However, the 6th century painter of this scene has left Atalanta out of the picture.

The heroic Alcestis, having volunteered to die in place of her husband Admetus, prepares for her journey to the Underworld. The scene is carved in high relief on a section of a marble column.

Opposite, top:
A Roman mosaic of the 4th century A.D. Orpheus sits among wild creatures, charming them with his playing.

Bottom:
A marvellously naturalistic relief of one of the Muses, now in the Archaeological Museum, Istanbul. The Muses probably originated, like the nymphs, as water spirits, but they became associated with literary and musical inspiration. Their numbers varied. There were three at Mount Helicon and at Delphi, seven in Lesbos, and ultimately it was agreed there were nine.

entirely happy, but the boar was duly sighted and, though it killed two of the party, it was wounded by Atalanta and finished off by Meleager himself. Meleager then presented the body of the creature to Atalanta, whom he loved, and this brought the simmering discontent to the surface. Atalanta's presence had aroused criticism at the start, and Meleager's gesture provoked angry criticism. Losing his temper, Meleager attacked and killed his two chief critics, who happened to be his uncles. (In other versions, the deaths occurred during a civil war).

Now when Meleager was born, the Fates told his mother that he would live only as long as a certain branch, then smouldering on the fire, was not burnt away. She took the branch off the fire and hid it, but when she heard how Meleager had killed her brothers she retrieved it and threw it on the flames. Meleager at once died and, much as his mother regretted her action, descended to Tartaros, where Heracles met him and promised to marry his sister.

The maiden who had been the cause of the trouble on the Calydonian Boar Hunt had a curious history herself. She had been abandoned as a child and suckled by a bear, until found by some herdsmen. As a loyal follower of Artemis, she would not take a husband; moreover, she had been told that if she did she would turn into an animal. Atalanta was an extremely fast runner, and to discourage suitors she said she would only marry a man who could beat her in a sprint.

Eventually, a young man named Melanion, not a fast runner but a crafty thinker, contrived to win Atalanta. Through Aphrodite, who naturally disapproved of stern chastity, he obtained some golden apples, and when he took his test against Atalanta's fleetness, he rolled the apples in her path to delay her – for she could not resist turning aside to pick them up. Thus Melanion won the test (it seems obvious that Atalanta was not reluctant to lose) and the hand of Atalanta. But the prophecy did come true. The couple offended Zeus, apparently by making love while within sacred precincts, and he turned them into lions.

Another of the party in the Calydonian Boar Hunt was Admetus, King of Pherae, the friend of Apollo. His friendship with the god began when Apollo, in expiation for the crime of killing Cecrops, spent a year as Admetus' herdsman. Admetus' respectful treatment of his exalted farm-hand produced excellent results in the fertility of his herd and, more important, helped to gain him the beautiful Alcestis as a wife. The task set for the suitors of Alcestis by her father was to drive a chariot drawn by a wild boar and a lion. With Apollo's aid, Admetus completed the required circuit with his unruly team, and so gained the hand of Alcestis. But when he entered the bridal chamber on his wedding night, he was horrified to discover, instead of a comely maiden, a bed full of hissing snakes. For some reason Admetus, when offering sacrifices to the gods before the wedding, had omitted Artemis, whose hostile view of matrimony made her appeasement particularly advisable, and this was the revenge of the goddess. Apollo's good offices were again invoked, the sacrifice belatedly made, and Artemis lifted her spell.

Apollo did Admetus another good turn when he discovered that the king was due to die soon, but that he could go on living if a member of his family volunteered to die instead. When the day came, Apollo delayed the Fates by making them drunk, while Admetus begged his elderly parents to do the decent thing. Their reactions were understandably negative, but Alcestis generously agreed to die instead of her husband, and took poison.

This rather sad and unsatisfactory tale has a happy ending. For to the joy of Admetus, Alcestis came back from the dead. Accounts of how she did so vary. One version, probably a late one as it implies recognition of the status of women, says that Persephone considered the whole proceedings disgraceful, and sent Alcestis back to earth. Another, adopted by Euripides, says that the good deed was done by Heracles, who happened to call on Admetus at this time and learned what had happened. Wielding his club of wild olive, he waited at the grave, and when Thanatos, the demon of death, or Hades himself, appeared to carry Alcestis off, Heracles forced him to give her up.

Admetus was a cousin of Jason and took part in the Quest for the Golden Fleece. Another of Jason's cousins, Melampus, though not usually included among the Argonauts, figures in an interesting story of his own.

Melampus, who is sometimes regarded as the first physician, is a minor figure, but a particularly attractive one. Not only did he enjoy some prophetic powers, taught by Apollo whom he happened to meet one day, but he understood the language of animals. He had acquired this gift through kindness: he had once rescued a nest of young snakes from death and, in gratitude, they licked out his ears with their tongues. Melampus employed this gift to assist his brother, Bias.

Bias was desperately in love with the lovely Pero, but her father had set for her many suitors a task even harder than that set by the father of Alcestis. The successful candidate was required to drive off the cattle of King Phylacus, which were guarded by a miraculously formidable watchdog. Melampus made the attempt on his brother's behalf, but was caught—as, indeed, he had intended—and put in prison.

Hypnos (Sleep) and Thanatos (Death) carrying the body of Sarpedon, a Trojan prince, from the battlefield to prevent Patroclus despoiling the corpse. The presence of blessed Sleep was a privilege few enjoyed – Thanatos alone waited for most mortals – but Sarpedon was a son of Zeus.

Right:
A famous red-figure krater, now in Berlin, with Orpheus singing, surrounded by attentive listeners in Thracian dress.

In his cell he heard two weary woodworms complaining of the labour of gnawing through a roof-beam, and rejoicing that the beam was about to fall at last. Melampus at once set up a clamour and demanded a new cell. Phylacus agreed, laughing, but his laughing stopped when the beam actually fell. So impressed was he with Melampus' powers that he agreed to let him go, and take the cattle, if he would cure his son Iphiclus of impotence.

Melampus agreed, and while he was preparing a sacrifice to Apollo, he overheard two vultures discussing the patient: how he had been frightened as a child by the sight of his father carrying a bloody knife, and how he could be cured of the impotence (which had been caused when Phylacus, hastening to comfort his son, had unthinkingly stuck the knife into a sacred tree), by application of rust from the knife, still in place in the tree. Thus Melampus cured Iphiclus; he gained the cattle, and Bias gained Pero.

Melampus, whose name suggests a possibly African origin, appears in a less attractive light in another myth, in which he withheld his power to cure an outbreak of madness until the king of the country promised to divide his realm into three, one-third to be kept, one-third for Melampus, and one-third for Bias.

Orpheus, although he sailed with the Argonauts, was not a hero in the usual sense of Greek mythology. At the same time he was not a god—indeed he is a difficult figure to categorize. His chief importance seems to have been religious: the mysteries of Orpheus were concerned with death and salvation—but they remain mysterious. Orpheus is also linked with Dionysus, and is often described as one of his followers; he came from Thrace, the country most closely associated with the wine-god. There are, of course, many theories about Orpheus: that he was a real person and a king of Thrace, that he was not one man but an amalgam of several, and so on. In myth, however, he figures chiefly as a great musician, and as the husband of Eurydice.

The mother of Orpheus was Calliope, or possibly another of the Muses. His father was either a river god, or a Thracian king, or possibly Apollo. Certainly, the instrument that he played so beautifully was the lyre, Apollo's instrument. It is sometimes said that Orpheus invented the lyre, or that he was responsible for increasing the number of strings from seven to nine. His playing and singing were so fine that all nature was charmed by them, and his chief function on the voyage of the Argonauts was to calm the elements and to drown the deadly songs of the Sirens with his own, even more beautiful singing.

Although the story of Orpheus' descent into the Underworld is known chiefly through late writers, notably Ovid, it is generally agreed that the story is very old.

Eurydice (like many names of individuals in mythology, it implies an office or quality, in this case possibly 'queen') was the beautiful wife of Orpheus. She was desired by Aristaeus, from whom she was forced to flee. In her flight she stepped on a snake, whose poisonous bite killed her. Orpheus decided to go down to the Underworld in an effort to bring her back. The beautiful playing of his lyre eased his way, for neither Charon nor Cerberus offered any resistance, and Hades himself was charmed. So much so that he agreed to let Eurydice return. He made only one condition. Orpheus should precede her on the journey out of Tartaros and should not for a moment turn to look at Eurydice until they were back on earth. Orpheus obeyed, until he had almost reached the light when, suddenly fearing that it had all been a trick, he looked behind him. The figure of Eurydice rapidly faded from his sight, the gates of hell closed against him, and he returned to the world alone.

In his distress Orpheus avoided company, but especially (or only) the company of women. Eventually, he was torn to pieces by Thracian women in a Dionysian orgy, perhaps because they resented his rejection of women, whether through jealousy, or hatred of Orpheus' homosexual relationships, or because he had revealed the secrets of the Underworld to men only, it would be difficult to say. Myths proliferated around the death of Orpheus. His head, singing of Eurydice, was thrown into a river and eventually floated to the island of Lesbos where, for a time, it acted as an oracle—even, according to one story, drawing suppliants away from Delphi.

The death of Orpheus at the hands of women in a Dionysiac frenzy. Red-figure jar (lekythos) in the Boston Museum of Fine Arts.

The Theban Cycle

Certain groups or cycles of relatively self-contained legends, such as the Trojan war and its aftermath, provided a body of material upon which the imagination of successive generations of poets worked in classical times and, indeed, up to the present. One of these was the so-called Theban Cycle, in which the major character is Oedipus, a tragic hero of almost cosmic dimensions. The poet chiefly associated with the Theban Cycle is the great 5th-century B.C. tragic playwright, Sophocles.

In myth, the founder of Thebes was Cadmus, a hero probably of Near-Eastern origin, brother of Europa and of several others who bore names similarly of geographical significance. They were descended from Io, an early love of Zeus and possibly a local variant of Hera, subsequently identified with the Egyptian Isis. But to delve deeply into the mythological genealogies, which are complicated by the frequent tendency of parents to have fifty children each, is not necessary here. We may begin with the search of Cadmus and his brothers for their sister Europa, after she had been abducted by Zeus in the form of a bull. In that search, Cadmus himself followed a wandering cow. One version says that he had consulted the oracle at Delphi, who advised him to forget about finding Europa and to build a city wherever the cow stopped.

The cow wandered until it came to the future site of Thebes, where it lay down, and Cadmus founded his city which was at first called Cadmeia. He wanted to sacrifice the cow to Athena, and sent some of his men to draw water for the sacrifice from a nearby stream. But the stream was sacred to Ares and was guarded by a great dragon, which killed most of Cadmus' men. Cadmus himself soon despatched the dragon, and Athena then appeared, advising him to sow the teeth of the dragon in the ground. He did so, and from the dragon's teeth sprang a host of armed warriors. They began to fight among themselves, either spontaneously or because Cadmus, thinking they looked too dangerous, lobbed a stone among them, and at the end of the battle only five warriors were left alive. From those five the great families of Thebes were descended.

However, Cadmus had offended Ares by killing his dragon, and had to undergo a period of servitude as penance. Thereafter, he married the daughter of Ares and Aphrodite, Harmonia (perhaps an unlikely name for the product of such a union), in a gorgeous wedding ceremony attended by the gods and the Muses. Cadmus' wedding present to his bride was a marvellous necklace, made by Hephaestus, and a splendid robe; these gifts figured later in the fight of the Seven against Thebes.

The subsequent affairs of Cadmus and Harmonia are of peripheral

interest only. They went to Illyria, were changed into snakes, and finally reached Elysium. The dynasty founded by Cadmus at Thebes was named after his grandson, Labdacus; in some sources, Cadmus had no sons and Labdacus was the founder of the dynasty.

Labdacus died when his son Laius (father of Oedipus) was a baby, and a nobleman of Thebes (one of those descended from the dragon's teeth) made himself king. His name was Nycteus, and he had a daughter, Antiope, whom Zeus seduced. Fearing her father's anger, Antiope fled from Thebes and sought safety with King Euopeus, at Sicyon in the Peloponnese. Nycteus committed suicide, after persuading his brother, Lycus, to punish Antiope. Lycus attacked Sicyon, killed Euopeus, and dragged Antiope back to Thebes. On the way she gave birth to twin sons, Amphion and Zethus, who were exposed on a hillside but rescued by herdsmen. Twenty years later, Antiope escaped from her harsh imprisonment in Thebes and was reunited with her sons, the musician Amphion and the warrior Zethus. They led a revolution in which Lycus was killed along with his unpleasant queen, Dirce, who had been especially cruel to Antiope. Amphion and Zethus then ruled Thebes jointly until they died, when Laius regained his throne. This briefly, was the dynastic background to the birth of Oedipus.

A curse hung over the house of Laius. Some say it had been pronounced by Pelops, whose son, Chrysippus, Laius had fallen in love with, and kidnapped while he was supposed to be teaching the boy to drive a chariot. Alternatively, he was warned by an oracle that if he had a son, that son would kill him. Thus, when Laius' wife, Jocasta, gave birth to a boy, the baby was abandoned in the wilderness, with a spike driven through his feet. This wound gave him his name, Oedipus, 'Swollen-foot'.

Europa about to mount the bull, which is of course Zeus and will carry her off. Her brother Cadmus went in search of her, and eventually arrived at the spot which became the city of Thebes.

Cadmus, here armed with the Gorgon shield, kills the dragon from whose teeth will spring the warriors of Thebes. Black-figure painting from a vessel in the Louvre.

The abandoned baby was found by Corinthian shepherds, who brought him to their king, Polybus. The wife of Polybus was unable to have children of her own, and therefore the royal couple welcomed the foundling. Oedipus grew up at Corinth thinking that Polybus was his father. Not until he was a young man did a chance remark lead him to doubt it, and sent him to Delphi to consult the oracle. At Delphi he was warned that it was his fate to kill his father and marry his mother. Still ignorant of his true parentage, the horrified Oedipus resolved never to go near Corinth again.

He resumed his travels, and not long afterwards—according to tradition at a place near Phocis where three roads met—he encountered an elderly man accompanied by attendants. A quarrel over the right of way ended in a fight, in which Oedipus killed his opponents. He continued on his way to Thebes, not knowing that the first part of the oracle's warning had already come to pass; for the traveller on the road had been Laius.

He found Thebes in disarray. The king had vanished on a journey, presumably murdered by robbers, and Jocasta's brother, Creon, had taken over. But, in addition, Thebes was being persecuted by a monster with a twisted intellect, the Sphinx, a winged creature with the body of a lion and the head of a woman. The Sphinx propounded a riddle, which no one could answer, and the penalty for failure was to be eaten by the Sphinx. Oedipus, however, solved the riddle, and the Sphinx in frustrated rage dashed herself to pieces in a ravine.

According to tradition, the riddle of the Sphinx was this. What creature walks sometimes on four legs, sometimes on two, sometimes on three, and is weakest when it is supported by the most legs? The answer that Oedipus gave was a man, for he crawls on all fours as a child, walks upright in his prime, and hobbles with a stick when he is old.

So impressed were the people of Thebes by Oedipus' destruction of the Sphinx that they wanted him to be their king. Some say that this office was the reward promised by Creon to anyone who could defeat the Sphinx. To become king, it was necessary to marry the dead king's queen, which Oedipus did. Thus, still unknowing, Oedipus fulfilled the second part of the oracle's prophecy, that he would marry his mother.

In an old version of the legend, the truth of the identity of Oedipus was then revealed by the gods, or by the scars on his feet, whereupon Jocasta hanged herself, while Oedipus apparently continued to rule in Thebes for some time until he died, possibly in battle.

A more dramatic story is told by Sophocles and later writers. A plague fell upon Thebes, and Creon journeyed to Delphi seeking help from the oracle, who said that the plague would not end until the death of Laius was avenged. Oedipus himself swore a fierce oath against the unknown murderer. At the same time, a messenger who came from Corinth to invite Oedipus to be king there (for Polybus had died) revealed that he was not the child of Polybus and his queen and need therefore have no fear of the oracle's prophecy. But Oedipus began to investigate his origins, and finally learned the truth from the very man who had abandoned him as a baby in the wilderness. In mortification he put out his own eyes, while Jocasta committed suicide. Then, according to the Athenian version, Oedipus was banished and Creon once more ruled in Thebes. The stricken hero, accompanied by his daughter Antigone, wandered to Attica, where he was welcomed by Theseus and later died.

In another, more likely, version, Oedipus never left Thebes. He remained a recluse, attended by his sons, Eteocles and Polynices.

On these sons he pronounced a curse – either because they rejected him or disobeyed him in some minor, but ritualistically significant, way. The burden of his curse was that they should quarrel and kill each other. This curse introduces the next stage of the Theban cycle, for it was Oedipus' last important act.

After his death, his curse was fulfilled. Eteocles and Polynices quarrelled over which one of them should rule Thebes. Eventually they decided to rule alternate years. Eteocles took the first year and Polynices went into a twelve-month exile; but predictably, when his time was up, Eteocles showed himself unwilling to surrender the throne, and civil war became inevitable.

During his year of exile, Polynices had gone to Argos, ruled at that time by Adrastus. This king had been told, rather puzzlingly, that his two daughters would marry, respectively, a lion and a boar. When Polynices came to Argos, he was wearing a lion-skin, and Adrastus saw in him a prospective son-in-law. Another young man, Tydeus, son of the king of Calydon, arrived in Argos at the same time as Polynices and in similar circumstances. His garment was the skin of a boar (or that was the device on his shield), and he was clearly intended for the second daughter of Adrastus. The two young exiles got into an argument, but Adrastus made peace between them and promised to help restore them to their thrones. The two marriages took place. Polynices' wedding present to his bride, Argeia, was the necklace of Harmonia.

Amphion and Zethus preparing to build the walls of Thebes. Amphion drew the stones after him by the music of his magic lyre: Zethus fitted them into place.

An army was gathered to attack Thebes and restore Polynices to the throne. Thebes had seven gates, and one commander was detailed to attack each gate. These were the Seven against Thebes: Adrastus, Polynices, Tydeus; two Argive heroes named Capaneus and Hippomedon; Parthenopaeus, who was the son of Melanion and Atalanta; and Amphiaraus, who was the son of a seer and had inherited some of his father's abilities. Amphiaraus, indeed, knew that the expedition was doomed and that if he went on he would not return. But his wife compelled him to go: she had been bribed by Polynices with Harmonia's necklace (which he had retrieved from Argeia), and before he left, Amphiaraus made his children swear that they would avenge him by killing their mother and fighting against Thebes themselves.

The expedition set off. It passed through Nemea, where it was responsible for founding the Nemean games, and in an open battle the Thebans were forced to retreat to their city. But when they attacked Thebes itself, the Argive-Calydonian allies were utterly routed. Of the Seven, only Adrastus survived. Tydeus might have been saved by Athena, who had always shown an interest in him and had been impressed by his exploit in killing all fifty members of a Theban ambush, but he revolted her by eating the brains of his adversary, Melanippus, and he died with the rest. Capaneus unwisely boasted that Zeus himself would not stop him breaching the Theban defences, at which he was struck down by a thunderbolt. Another thunderbolt was probably responsible for opening the hole in the ground into which the chariot of Amphiaraus fatally plunged as he was fleeing. The last to die was Polynices, who fought a mortal duel with his brother, Eteocles.

The death of the two brothers left Creon once more supreme in Thebes. He offended the gods by ordering that the bodies of the dead should be left to rot where they lay. This was sacrilege, and invited divine retribution which, though delayed for ten years, was certain.

A spectator of the battle of the Seven against Thebes was Antigone, daughter of Oedipus, who had returned to the city after her father's death. Her story, like that of Oedipus himself, emphasizes the grim message of the Theban Cycle that fate is arbitrary and unkind.

Antigone had watched her brothers fight and kill each other. Eteocles had received a proper burial, but Polynices was left to lie where he fell, according to Creon's order. Antigone recognized a higher duty than obedience to the king—to perform the rite of burial. She went secretly and scattered dust over the body of Polynices, but her action was discovered and Creon sentenced her to death. She was buried alive in an underground chamber.

Creon's action was doubly harsh since Antigone was beloved of, or married to, his own son, Haemon. He attempted to rescue her but found that she had already hanged herself, whereupon Haemon committed suicide over her body. (Euripides has a somewhat happier version, in which Haemon and Antigone escaped and had a son, though they later returned to Thebes and were killed).

Another resident in Thebes at the time of the assault of the Seven was the seer, Tiresias. Unlike many others in Thebes, he is a figure closer to myth than to legend, for his curious early experiences had involved him in the family squabbles of the gods, and he reputedly lived for nearly two hundred years. Like many other Greek seers (including, by tradition, Homer himself), Tiresias was blind. Once he had stumbled on Athena taking a bath, and the goddess had thrown water at him which took away his sight.

Another explanation of Tiresias' blindness tells how he came upon two snakes copulating and killed the female, whereupon he turned

Oedipus thoughtfully contemplating the Sphinx, whose riddle he was able to answer. From a 5th-century kylix.

Opposite:
Amphion and Zethus revenge themselves on the cruel queen Dirce by binding her to the horns of a wild bull. A Roman copy of a Hellenistic marble. From the Baths of Caracalla.

into a woman. He remained female for some time until he found two more snakes in the same situation and killed the male, which turned him back into a man. His unique experience made him the obvious person to deliver a judgment when Zeus and Hera were arguing over which partner, male or female, derives most enjoyment from sex. Tiresias replied that sex was ten times more enjoyable for the female, an answer that annoyed Hera so much she struck him blind. In compensation, Zeus gave him the gifts of prophecy and a long life.

During the war of the Seven against Thebes, Tiresias advised that for the city to be saved it was necessary to sacrifice one of the nobility to Ares' sacred dragon. Menoiceus, a son of Creon, volunteered to be the victim, stabbing himself on the battlements and thus saving the city.

Ten years after the annihilation of the Seven, Adrastus led another expedition against Thebes, its leaders consisting of the sons of the Seven (all this may suggest the world of 'Western' films, a more modern mythology but one which offers fruitful comparisons). They are known as the Epigoni, the 'younger generation'.

This time the result was different. The Epigoni defeated the Thebans and restored Thersander, son of Polynices. Advised by Tiresias, the Thebans stealthily evacuated their women and children under cover of night: they travelled by waggon, following Cadmus' route to Illyria. Tiresias went with them and died on the way. The

Parnassus: the road eastward from Delphi, to Thebes and Athens. This was the way Oedipus travelled after consulting the oracle. The road from Phocis joins it from the north-west, making the place where three roads met and for the fatal encounter with Laius.

only member of the Epigoni who was killed in the fighting was the son of Adrastus, and the King of Argos himself, now an old man, died of grief on the return journey, mounting his own funeral pyre in fulfilment of a prophecy of Apollo.

Meanwhile, the necklace of Harmonia retained its capacity to cause disaster. Alcmeon, son of Amphiaraus and leader of the Epigoni, killed his mother in accordance with the oath extracted from him by his father when the latter had departed with the Seven against Thebes. The murder brought the Furies (Erinyes) down upon him, and he was driven away, coming eventually to Psophis, where he married the king's daughter, Arsinoe. But he was still persecuted, and famine fell upon the country. Alcmeon left to seek a land which had not existed when he committed the murder, and thus he came to some off-shore islands formed from the deposits of the River Achelous.

There he married Callirhoe, daughter of the river god, but his new bride desired the famous necklace, which was still in Phocis. Alcmeon obtained it by saying that he was going to dedicate it to Apollo at Delphi, but his lie was discovered, and he was attacked and killed by the sons of the King of Psophis. The act was witnessed by Arsinoe, who did not know of Alcmeon's marriage to Callirhoe and had agreed to surrender the necklace, because she believed that by offering it at Delphi Alcmeon would finally rid himself of the vengeful Furies and return to her. So strongly did she protest that her father locked her in a chest and sent her a slave to Arcadia.

Callirhoe, learning of the death of Alcmeon, prayed to Zeus that her sons might reach manhood quickly and avenge their father. Zeus granted her wish, and the sons of Alcmeon killed the King of Psophis and all his family. Then they took the necklace of Harmonia and dedicated it to Apollo at Delphi, bringing the saga to an end (though there are later stories of the necklace being stolen from Delphi and predictably bringing disaster upon the thief).

Eteocles and Polynices dying after their fight outside the walls of Thebes. From an Italian alabaster urn, carved in relief.

The Epics

The Quest for the Golden Fleece

The journey, or quest, has its place in almost every mythology, and to the Greeks the greatest of all such stories was the Quest for the Golden Fleece. Like practically every other story, it is a mixture of elements, part religious, part political, part history, and part folk-lore. The travellers' objective – the Fleece itself – is of marginal importance. The legend of the Fleece was this.

Ino, the one-time nurse of Dionysus, who was later to be helpful to Odysseus, was married to Athamas. He already had two children, Phrixus and Helle, by a previous union with Nephele. Ino was jealous of her stepchildren and plotted to get rid of them by bribing messengers from Delphi to report that the oracle advised the sacrifice of the two children, in order to save the land from famine – a famine, incidentally, induced by Ino herself. Nephele, the real mother of the children, was a Cloud spirit, and she sent a golden ram to save them. They climbed on its back and it carried them off towards Colchis, beyond the Black Sea. Unfortunately, Helle fell off at the Dardanelles – or Hellespont – and only Phrixus survived to reach the refuge offered by King Aietes of Colchis. The ram was sacrificed to Zeus, and Phrixus hung up its fleece in a sacred grove guarded by a fierce dragon. Phrixus himself married the daughter of his protector, had several children by her, and eventually died at Colchis. All this, however, has little directly to do with Jason and his fellow Argonauts.

Jason, who came from Thessaly, was the grandson of Athamas and the nephew of King Pelias, who had seized the throne unlawfully from Jason's father. Pelias killed all likely opponents to his rule, and would have killed Jason too, but the child was taken away by his mother and brought up in the care of Chiron, the wise Centaur, who was the protector also of Achilles and several other heroes.

Years later, Jason came to Pelias' court at Iolcus to claim the kingdom that was rightfully his. Pelias was not at all pleased to see him, especially as he was wearing only one sandal, for Pelias had been warned to beware of a man thus idiosyncratically dressed. In fact, it appears to have been a custom in Aetolia to discard a sandal in order to get a better grip on muddy ground, but there was another explanation of Jason's one bare foot which Pelias would have found more ominous. On his journey to Iolcus, Jason had to cross a river, and finding an old woman there, he helped her across too, losing a sandal in the process. Safely across, the old woman revealed herself as none other than the goddess Hera. Already opposed to Pelias, who had failed to offer her appropriate sacrifices, she became henceforth the friend of Jason, who was also assisted by Athena, a goddess with a soft

Medea demonstrating to Pelias and his daughters how she can rejuvenate a ram. The gullible family was convinced, and Pelias went into Medea's pot, but far from being rejuvenated, he died.

Phrixos escaping from his stepmother with the aid of the golden-fleeced flying ram sent by his mother, Nephele, which carried him to Colchis.

spot for all heroes. But even without this knowledge, Pelias had every cause to fear Jason, and it was clever of him to get rid of his hero by sending him off on what he imagined would be a fatal journey. It is said that he tricked Jason into going by asking him what he would do if an oracle warned him that a certain man was destined to kill him, whereupon Jason rather thoughtlessly replied that he would send such a man to fetch the Golden Fleece at Colchis. Pelias' story that the country was afflicted by a curse which would not be lifted until the Fleece was regained, and his promise to give up the throne at that time, more or less compelled Jason to accept the challenge.

In spite of the dangerous nature of the task, many volunteered to accompany him. (As with Zeus' illegitimate children, one can detect a desire among great families to number an Argonaut among their ancestors which led retrospectively to the large size of Jason's company.) Among the fifty chosen, for instance, was Heracles, whom it is hard to imagine as a good team man. No doubt he was included because he was thought to be contemporary with Jason and thus could hardly be left out of such a heroic enterprise. Though Heracles proved a useful member of the expedition, he departed from it quite early, being left behind at the river Chius while he was searching for his youthful attendant, Hylas, who had been kidnapped by water-nymphs enchanted by his beauty.

Another unexpected member of the expedition – and, like Heracles, no doubt a late addition – was Orpheus, though he did no heavy rowing. Then there was Peleus, father of Achilles, several members of the Calydonian Boar Hunt, Castor and Pollux, and the sons of the North Wind, Calais and Zetes. Several heroes had special assignments, like Lynceus the look-out man and Tiphys the pilot.

A ship – the first longship – was built under Athena's guidance. The goddess was also responsible for the remarkable prow of the *Argo* which, being made of sacred oak, had the ability to speak. After a riotous feast, at which the lyre of Orpheus soothed several drunken quarrels, the *Argo* set out.

Below :
The story of the Quest of the Golden Fleece had many variants. Here, Athena looks on as the dragon, which has swallowed Jason, disgorges him.

Bottom :
Group portrait of the Argonauts, from a 5th-century krater in the Louvre. Among those present is Heracles, with his olive-wood club, and Athena is mingling with the heroes.

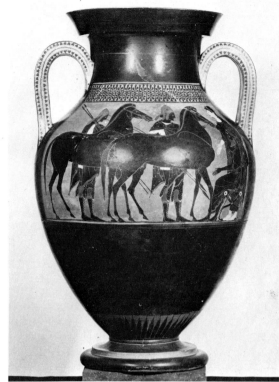

Castor and Pollux with their parents, Leda and Tyndareus.

Above, left:
Jason takes the Golden Fleece. Athena looks on with satisfaction and, at the right, the *Argo* is prepared for a quick getaway. There is no sign of Medea in this scene, which dates from 470–460 B.C.

Their first stop was the island of Lemnos, which they found to be populated entirely by women. Having at some time offended Aphrodite, the women of Lemnos had been afflicted with an unpleasant smell, which drove their men to neglect them and seek other female company from the mainland. Incensed, the women planned a massive coup d'état, in which they slaughtered the whole male population. Only Hypsipyle showed any compassion, setting her elderly father adrift in a boat so that, with the help of Dionysus, he escaped. Finding that the Argonauts were not, as they first thought, enemies from Thrace, the women of Lemnos not surprisingly welcomed their visitors, and it appears that their foul smell had left them, for numerous children were begotten during the prolonged visit. Jason himself had several sons by Hypsipyle, but declined her offer of the vacant throne.

Having passed the Hellespont – normally barred to Greek ships by the Trojans – under cover of darkness, the Argonauts reached the land of the Dolionians just in time to take part in the wedding feast of King Cyzicus (son of Aeneas). They were attacked by some six-handed giants but drove them off. Unfortunately, a storm blew them back to land that night and the Dolionians, not recognizing their former guests in the dark, attacked them. In the fighting, Cyzicus was killed, and his bride committed suicide. It also transpired that the giants whom the Argonauts had killed were brothers of Rhea, and a further delay was caused by the need to propitiate the Earth goddess.

Good speed was made thereafter as Heracles proposed a rowing competition which, needless to say, he won. But at the moment when his last rival, Jason, finally cracked, Heracles broke his oar. To get wood for a new one was the reason for the *Argo*'s stop at the River Chius, where Heracles was left behind frantically searching for his missing Hylas. (When Heracles next met Calais and Zetes, who had persuaded their comrades to leave without him, he killed them both; their gravestones on the island of Tenos sway when the north wind blows.)

Medea, certain that Jason will abandon her for the princess of Corinth, Glauce, formulates her revenge, which will involve the murder of her own children. The old man at the left is a tutor. A wall painting from Pompeii.

Above, right:
Glauce, centre, dies of the poisoned robe beside her father, Creon, with Jason powerless to save her. Below, he is too late to prevent Medea killing their children and escaping in a serpentine chariot.

Opposite:
The goddess Athena was, like Hera, unequivocally on the side of the Achaeans in the war against Troy. In this detail from an Etruscan vase she has just witnessed the death of Patroclus (bottom left).

On the island of Bebrycos, the Argonauts encountered King Amycus, who insisted on a boxing match with all visitors. But Pollux was a boxer of exceptional skill and power and he briskly disposed of Amycus with a blow that cracked his skull and killed him. The people of Bebrycos then attacked the Argonauts, but were swiftly routed, and the place was sacked. However, a sacrifice had to be made to Poseidon, as Amycus had been his son.

The next ruler the Argonauts encountered was a far more interesting character, Phineus, a blind seer, ruler of Salmydessus on the western shore of the Black Sea. Various reasons for his blindness are put forward, one being that he had offended the gods by his accurate prophecies. It is said that Zeus offered him the choice of blindness or a short life, and that his choice offended Helios, who sent the Harpies to plague him. These were disgusting winged female creatures who, whenever food was put in front of Phineus, came hurtling down and snatched it away, or smothered it with their droppings. Jason was anxious to get advice from Phineus, but first agreed to get rid of the Harpies. A feast was prepared and, as the Harpies came down upon it, Calais and Zetes, the sons of the North Wind, rose into the air with swords brandished and put them to flight.

Of the advice that Phineus gave Jason, the most immediately useful was a trick for passing the Symplegades. These were dangerous rocks which tended to clash together unpredictably as a ship was passing between them. Phineus said that a dove should be sent through first and if it passed safely then the ship might follow. Jason followed this advice, and the dove flew between the rocks, only losing one of its tail feathers as they clashed together. The *Argo* followed, and lost one board from the stern as the rocks clashed behind it.

After some mishaps, including the death of Typhis the pilot and of Idmon, a seer who had foretold his own end while hunting a boar, they reached the island of Ares where the Stymphalian birds had taken

Pelops and Hippodamia: preparations for the chariot race that brought a curse on the house of Pelops. The central figure is Zeus with, on his right, Oenomaus, Sterope and Myrtilus the charioteer. On the left of Zeus are Pelops, Hippodamia and Sphaeros (Pelops' charioteer). East pediment of the temple of Zeus, now in the Olympia Museum.

Opposite, top:
The Judgment of Paris, which led indirectly to the Trojan War. Hermes leads the three goddesses, Athena, Hera and Aphrodite to Paris, who appears, surrounded by goats and playing the lyre, as a shepherd.

Bottom:
The sacrifice of Iphigenia, the crime which renewed the curse on the house of Atreus and Agamemnon. The goddess Artemis sends a deer to take the place of Iphigenia and spirits her away to be her priestess at Tauris. She is eventually reunited with her brother Orestes.

refuge after being expelled by Heracles. They seem to have become less fearsome since then, for the Argonauts frightened them away by banging their shields. On this island, the *Argo* picked up two new members, the sons of Phrixus, who had been shipwrecked there while trying to return to Greece. Other replacements were three young men who had accompanied Heracles on his expedition against the Amazons and so far had not made much progress homeward. Soon after that, the Argonauts arrived at Colchis.

From this point on, the legend deteriorates somewhat. For one thing, there are so many variations to the narrative that it is difficult to extract a coherent story. There are also additions which seem to be dragged in from other myths, and while Jason himself remains a hero, events become darker and meaner, more like sub-Jacobean tragedy than Greek epic. Medea is a thoroughly unpleasant character, without redeeming features (though Zeus admired her spirit).

At Colchis, Aietes was not unnaturally reluctant to surrender the Golden Fleece. He did not actually refuse, which anyway would have been extremely unwise given the military capacities of the Argonauts, but he insisted that a test would have to be performed first, and it was a test that no one was supposed to pass. One of the Argonauts— Jason as it turned out—had to plough a large field with two bulls, and then to sow in the field the dragon's teeth which have already appeared before in the story of Cadmus; some of them had since come into the possession of Aietes. The catch was that the bulls had been made by Hephaestus; they were of bronze and breathed fire.

Aietes was the brother of Circe the enchantress, and he had a daughter with the same gifts, Medea. On Jason's arrival at Colchis, Medea had fallen in love with him, a very useful attachment as it proved, which had been engineered by Hera. Medea was able to equip Jason to pass the test that Aietes had set him, on condition that Jason took her as his wife, which he agreed to do. She gave him a lotion that made him proof to the fiery breath of the bronze bulls; he mastered them, and ploughed the field as Aietes had ordered. Then, aping Cadmus, he sowed the dragon's teeth and threw a stone among the warriors who sprouted, which set them fighting. This time there were no survivors.

Then Aietes proved his falseness by refusing to part with the Fleece, and laying plans to attack the Argonauts and burn their ship. Medea again came to the rescue, and led Jason and his comrades stealthily to the sacred place where the Fleece was hanging. The dragon guarding it, which was larger than the *Argo,* had been born from the blood of Typhon, the gigantic monster overcome by Zeus, but Medea put it to sleep. Jason crept up, took the Fleece from the oak tree where it hung, and all slipped away to the ship. Aietes pursued them hotly, but Medea delayed him by scattering behind the

A council of the gods during the Trojan War. Left to right, Ares, Aphrodite, Artemis and Apollo. From the frieze below the east pediment of the Syphnian treasury at Delphi.

Opposite, top :
This bronze figure, like most large classical bronzes that survive, was recovered from the sea in modern times. The subject is an idealised youth. The Greeks would have imagined heroes like Achilles cast in such a mould.

Bottom :
Odysseus tries to persuade Philoctetes, whom the Greeks abandoned when he was suffering from an incurable wound, to accompany him to Troy, bringing the bow of Heracles. Neoptolemus, son of Achilles, appears behind Odysseus. Silver cup in the National Museum, Copenhagen.

Argo the severed limbs of her young brother, Apsyrtus, whom she had killed for that purpose, knowing Aietes would stop to recover the pieces.

No geographical sense can be made of the homeward voyage of the *Argo*. The whole legend undoubtedly enshrines an actual voyage, but not enough authentic details survived for a course or purpose to be ascribed to it. The bards who told the story to successive generations probably added new places, seas and rivers as fancy took them and as geographical knowledge expanded. (There is some evidence that in the earliest versions of the Quest, the objective of the Argonauts was not in the Black Sea at all, but in the Adriatic.) Among major rivers that the Argonauts are said to have rowed along during their homeward voyage were the Danube, the Rhine, the Don, and the Po. One account had them circumnavigating the British Isles, which would have been not only a remarkably long way round but also far beyond the known world of 13th-century B.C. Greece.

However, certain episodes on the return voyage were widely repeated, such as the successful passage of the Sirens, where only one member of the crew, Butes, found the Sirens' singing more beguiling than that of Orpheus. He jumped into the sea, but was rescued by Aphrodite, whose lover he became. At some stage, Jason and Medea, following the advice uttered by the speaking prow of the *Argo*, visited the island of Circe to be purified for the murder of Apsyrtus. During a diversion in Libya they encountered Triton (or one of the Tritons), who towed the ship down a river back to the Mediterranean, and gave a lump of earth to Euphemus, one of the Argonauts, as a sign of his future sovereignty of the land. The earth later fell into the sea and became the island of Thera, which was colonized by Euphemus' descendants. In Crete they had some trouble with another of Hephaestus' robots, the bronze giant Talos, who used to walk round the island three times a day burning up all who approached, or hurling rocks at them. Medea divined his weak point, a vein in the heel sealed by a metal plug, and having put him into a trance, removed the plug and so killed him. Leaving Crete, the *Argo* was caught in a storm, but Apollo came to their aid by revealing an island where they could shelter. Finally the Argonauts reached Iolcus with the Golden Fleece.

Pelias proved unwilling to keep his part of the bargain. He had not expected to see Jason again and, some say, had killed the hero's parents during his absence. Jason and his comrades planned to raise forces against the fickle monarch, but Medea promised to capture the city single-handed. She gained entry to the palace by claiming to be the goddess Artemis, and persuaded Pelias' daughter to cut their father in pieces and boil him in a cauldron, as this would make him young again. Alcestis, who later married Admetus, declined to take part in this dubious ritual, but her sisters did, and thus brought Pelias' career to a grisly conclusion. However, after such a deed, the people would not accept Jason as king, and he and Medea went into exile in Corinth where, in some accounts, Jason reigned as king. Some time later, Jason became engaged to another woman, a daughter of King Creon. Medea sent the girl a wedding gown which, when she put it on, burst into flames and burned her alive. Creon also died in the fire. Pausing only to sacrifice her own children to Hera in exchange for a promise of immortality (or so said Euripides, whom later commentators accuse of accepting a Corinthian bribe to present this version of events), Medea fled. She spent some time in Athens, but was forced to leave that city after trying to poison Theseus, and later perhaps founded the land of Media, which was united with Colchis under her sway. Finally, some say, she went to Elysium, where she is the wife of Achilles. Jason's later years were less eventful. He wandered miserably from place to place and finally returned to Corinth. He was sitting in the shadow of the old *Argo*, contemplating suicide, when the prow broke off and fell on him, killing him outright.

Interlude between battles. Ajax, spears in his hand but his helmet and shield put aside, plays a board game with Achilles. From a 6th-century black-figured vase in the Vatican Museum.

The War against Troy

Those who took part in the Quest for the Golden Fleece belonged to the generation before that which fought the Trojan War; several of Jason's companions were the fathers of Trojan War heroes. The various legends and tales comprised in the story of the Trojan War and its immediate aftermath form the last period of the Greek heroic age, and there is a certain atmosphere of doom about them which perhaps foreshadows the eclipse of Mycenean civilization and the onset of the long 'dark age' following the Dorian invasions of about the 11th century B.C.

The best-known source for the legends of the Trojan War is the *Iliad* of Homer which must have been written down soon after Homer told his story in the 8th or 9th century and naturally includes some later elements; like all Greek mythology, it is a mixture of legend, myth and fairy tale. The *Iliad*, however, actually covers a very short period. It opens in the tenth year of the siege of Troy by the Greeks (or, as Homer calls them, Achaeans) and does not relate the final scenes. Its central character is Achilles, the leading warrior among the Greeks, and he was but one of the kings or chieftains who, in a loose, vaguely feudal federation, obeyed the call of Agamemnon to wage war against Troy. The background to the Trojan War is therefore concerned with the affairs of the dynasty headed by Agamemnon – the doomed House of Atreus.

Agamemnon was a descendant of Tantalus, a son of Zeus in some sources, and certainly a friend of the god as he was invited to Olympian banquets. But Tantalus disastrously offended the gods in one of several ways, the most popular account being that he invited them to

dinner and, not having enough food in the larder, served them his own son, Pelops, cut up in a stew. He appears to have thought the gods would not notice, but all of them did so and drew back in horror, except Demeter, who was preoccupied by her grief over the loss of Persephone and ate part of Pelops' shoulder. For his fearful offence, Tantalus was punished in Tartaros by being suspended over a lake, with branches of fruit hanging above his head. He was wracked with thirst and hunger, but whenever he reached down towards the water or up towards the fruit, they receded from his grasp.

Besides Pelops, who was restored with an ivory shoulder to replace what Demeter had eaten, Tantalus had an unfortunate daughter, Niobe. She unwisely claimed to be superior to Leto, because she had more children. But though Leto had only two, they were Apollo and Artemis, who avenged the insult to their mother by killing every one of Niobe's numerous brood. Niobe stood weeping over the bodies until she turned into a pillar of stone, from which water continued to flow.

If the fate of Tantalus and Niobe seems unduly harsh, Pelops was perhaps rather fortunate. He desired Hippodamia, daughter of Oenomaus, king of Pisa, and gained her by murder and treachery. The test that the suitors of Hippodamia were required to perform was to carry her off in a chariot while avoiding the spear of her pursuing father. Twelve suitors had tried and failed. Pelops bribed Myrtilus, the king's coachman, to tamper with the linchpin of Oenomaus' chariot wheel, with the result that the king was thrown out at full gallop and killed. Then Pelops murdered Myrtilus rather than pay the promised bribe. Pelops ruled the whole of the Peloponnese, which takes its name from him.

The famous Lion Gate at Mycenae, the main entrance to the citadel, built in the 14th century B.C. According to the myths Agamemnon's chariot passed under this massive structure when he returned victorious from Troy.

The sons of Pelops were Atreus and Thyestes, who were doomed by the evil brought upon the family by the crimes of their father and the dying curse of Myrtilus. The brothers were rivals for the throne of Mycenae, which Atreus gained when Thyestes was tricked into promising to surrender his claim if the sun should go backwards. Zeus, who supported Atreus and had prompted him to extract this promise, then made the sun go backwards. This was the only time the sun has ever set in the east. Atreus later discovered that Thyestes had been sleeping with his wife, but dissembled his anger, pretending to be reconciled with his brother. He invited him to a feast, but what he served up was the bodies of Thyestes' children.

The feud was carried on into the next generation. Thyestes, in exile, raped his own daughter, Pelopia, while in disguise, and the product of their union was a son, Aegisthus. Atreus had two sons, Agamemnon, King of Mycenae, and Menelaus, King of Sparta.

The sons of Atreus were married to two sisters, Clytemnestra and Helen, daughters of Leda whom Zeus had seduced in the form of a swan. It is usually said that Helen was a daughter of Zeus but that Clytemnestra's father was Leda's mortal husband. Leda was also the mother of Castor and Pollux, the heavenly twins, of whom Pollux at least was the son of Zeus and therefore immortal: that is why it is said that, after Castor was killed in a battle, Zeus granted the request of Pollux that he might remain with his brother and allowed them to spend alternate days in heaven and hell.

Helen was courted by many suitors, and married Menelaus by her own choice. For some time they lived happily together, and had a daughter, Hermione. Then, when Menelaus was away from home, the Trojan prince, Paris, appeared on the scene and abducted Helen, with or without her consent.

The suicide of Ajax. He aspired to the armour of Achilles after that leader was killed. But it was awarded to Odysseus, and Ajax's wrath turned to insanity and he took his own life. Etruscan bronze.

Right :
This red-figure painting of the late 6th century illustrates the difficult courtship of Peleus. Thetis was annoyed at being betrothed to a mere mortal when she wanted Zeus, and tried various wiles to put him off. But Peleus, a good wrestler, persevered, and eventually the couple married and produced Achilles.

This abduction, which resulted in the Trojan War, was actually the indirect result of a dissension in the family of the gods. At a banquet on Olympus, Eris (Strife) tossed a golden apple among the company labelled 'For the Fairest'. Inevitably, an argument began over who qualified for the apple, the leading claimants being Hera, Athena and Aphrodite. To give a decision, Zeus summoned Paris, the most handsome mortal alive and the son of King Priam of Troy. Paris gave the prize to Aphrodite, not necessarily because she deserved it but because she had bribed him with a promise that she would get him the most beautiful woman on earth as his wife. This turned out to be Helen, and it was with the help of Aphrodite that Paris seized Helen from Sparta and carried her back to Troy.

When the crime was discovered, Agamemnon, the brother of Menelaus, promised to raise a great expedition against Troy to retrieve Helen and punish the Trojans. The suitors of Helen, who had included nearly all the kings of Greece, had sworn to support the man whom Helen chose, and by and by they assembled for Agamemnon's expedition at Aulis. Not all were willing, however. In Ithaca, Odysseus pretended to be mad by ploughing his land with an ox and an ass yoked together, and sowing salt in the furrows. But Palamedes, sent to summon him, placed his infant son, Telemachus, in the way of the plough, and when Odysseus carefully avoided the boy his madness was exposed as a sham. There was some difficulty also in getting Achilles to Aulis. His mother, Thetis the Nereid, had disguised him as a girl and concealed him among the womenfolk of the King of Scyros. Odysseus and Diomedes went to find him, left their armour lying about in the women's quarters, and detected Achilles by the interest he showed in it.

Above:
The Wooden Horse—an early version in low relief on the neck of a 7th century amphora from Mykonos. Some of the Achaeans are handing down arms to their comrades.

Above, left:
Odysseus blinds the one-eyed giant, Polyphemus, with the burned and pointed staff of green olive wood. Detail from a painted amphora of the 7th century B.C.

123

A scene from a 6th-century black-figure krater: Hector bids farewell to Andromache, with various other characters of the Trojan War in attendance, including Paris and Helen, behind Andromache.

Achilles slays Penthesilea, the Amazon queen—an incident that does not occur in Homer. From a 5th century vase painting in the Antiken Sammlungen, Munich.

The start of the expedition was delayed by contrary winds, sent by Artemis who was offended with the Atreids. The seer Calchas was consulted, and his grim verdict was that Iphigenia, daughter of Agamemnon, would have to be sacrificed. But just as the girl was about to be ritually slaughtered, she was snatched away by Artemis, who provided a deer in her place.

Before they reached Troy, the Greeks, perhaps by mistake, landed in Mysia, where they were resisted by the king, Telephus, a son of Heracles. In the fighting, which was fairly brief, Telephus was wounded by Achilles. The wound refused to heal, and Telephus eventually went to Delphi to consult the oracle, who told him that his wound would be cured by what had caused it. So Telephus was forced to make another journey, to the Greek camp, where he sought out Achilles and was cured by the application of Achilles' spear to his wound.

Another incident involving a wound that refused to heal also delayed Agamemnon's expedition. This was suffered by Philoctetes, son of the man who had lit the funeral pyre of Heracles. He had inherited the arrows of Heracles, and one of them, dropped accidentally, left him with a suppurating wound. So loud were his groans or, alternatively, so bad the stench of the wound, that the Greeks abandoned him—temporarily, as it proved—on the island of Lemnos.

Finally the Greeks landed near Troy. An omen, in which a serpent had consumed nine birds in a tree, had been interpreted by Calchas as a sign that the war would last for nine years and that Troy would fall in ten; so a short campaign was not expected by anyone. The first man to leap ashore was Protesilaus, and this was a brave act for it had also been prophesied that the first man ashore would be the first to die. So it proved, for he was at once killed by Hector, another son of King Priam, who was to the Trojans what Achilles was to the Greeks—their finest warrior.

The first nine years of the siege can be passed over: nothing very significant happened. The Greeks raided a number of other towns in the area, and it was the result of one of these raids that provoked the Wrath of Achilles—the subject of Homer's *Iliad*.

Two girls were captured in the raid: Chryseis, who became the property of Agamemnon, and Briseis, her cousin, who was given to Achilles. Chryseis was the daughter of a priest of Apollo, who prayed to the god for vengeance. Apollo inflicted a plague on the Greeks, the reason for which was explained to them by Calchas. Relief, said the seer, could be obtained by returning the girl to her father. Reluctantly,

Achilles, supported by Athena, kills Hector. Artemis is less satisfied by the outcome of the famous duel. Detail from a painted amphora, 5th century B.C.

Left:
Priam, father of Hector, pleads with Achilles for the return of his son's body which lies despoiled beneath Achilles' couch. Red-figure krater now in Vienna.

Agamemnon consented, but he insisted that Briseis should be surrendered to him in place of Chryseis. Achilles, fascinated by his acquisition, was furious at being deprived of her. Angrily, he retired to his tent and refused to take any further part in the war.

Deprived of their best champion, the Greeks were driven back. Not even the valour of Ajax, who fought Hector to a draw in single combat, and Diomedes, the companion of Odysseus in a raid behind the Trojan lines, could withstand the Trojan advance. Agamemnon made overtures to Achilles through Odysseus – always the cunning diplomat – and others, but the son of Peleus was adamant. Hector broke through the Greek fortifications and set fire to one of the ships. At this disaster, Achilles relented sufficiently to permit his great friend Patroclus to borrow his armour and lead his followers, the Myrmidons, into the battle.

The appearance of Patroclus in the armour of Achilles turned the battle. Sarpedon, a Trojan son of Zeus, fell to Patroclus' own hand, and the Greeks might have breached the city walls if Apollo had not intervened – for several gods and goddesses took sides and actually took part in the fighting at Troy. While Patroclus was staggering from Apollo's blow, he was wounded by Euphorbus, and then Hector struck him a single blow which killed him. Menelaus, coming belatedly

Laocoön and his sons crushed by sea serpents. This remarkable group, considerably restored and now in the Vatican Museum, was discovered in quite recent times. It is a tour de force of Hellenic sculpture.

to his aid, killed Euphorbus but was repulsed by Hector. However, with the aid of Ajax, he defended Patroclus' body until night fell and they could carry it from the field–though the armour had been stripped off by Hector.

The death of Patroclus brought Achilles–in new armour hastily fashioned by Hephaestus–back into battle. His wrath was terrible, and none could stand against him. He split the Trojan forces in two, and sent them flying for the shelter of the city. At last, he came face to face with Hector, fought him three times around the walls, and killed him with a spear thrust through the chest. He tied his heels to his chariot, and drove back to camp dragging the body of Hector through the dust. Later, King Priam came secretly to Achilles, and begged for the body of his son for burial. Achilles, who knew that he was ordained to die soon himself, softened and consented, though for a substantial ransom. The funeral of Hector concluded the story told by Homer in the *Iliad*.

The Trojans were not without allies. From the north came Penthesileia and her Amazons, and from the south Memnon and his Ethiopians (both rather too exotic, perhaps, to have been included by Homer). They did good service, but both were killed by the fleet-footed Achilles. Some say that Achilles fell in love with Penthesileia even as he drove his sword through her. The ugly and unpleasant Thersites jeered at him for his weakness, and Achilles punched him so hard he killed him.

Not much has been heard of Paris, who was responsible for starting the war. He was, indeed, no warrior to compare with his brother Hector, and he was disliked by many in Troy who condemned his abduction of Helen. Yet it was Paris who finally killed Achilles–though Apollo guided his bow. The arrow struck Achilles in his only

The site of the Mycenaean shaft tombs. The double ring around the circumference protected the shaft graves of a royal dynasty of the 16th century B.C.

vulnerable part—the heel—the part (according to a later explanation) by which his mother Thetis had held him when she dipped him, as a baby, in the Styx to give him his invulnerability. The battle raged all day over the body of Achilles, but at last great Ajax, having killed Glaucus, brother of Sarpedon, brought the body home, while Odysseus protected his rear. Some later stories make Achilles immortal and place him in the Elysian Fields, married to Helen or (less amiably, one would imagine) to Medea.

Ajax himself soon followed Achilles. A terrific fighter, but not especially bright, Ajax with his giant shield is one of the most sympathetic of Homer's Achaeans. After the death of Achilles, it was debated who should receive his armour, the leading candidates being Ajax and Odysseus. The Trojan prisoners were asked who had caused them most trouble; they said Odysseus, so he was given the armour. In his disappointment, Ajax went temporarily mad, and rushed about killing sheep which he thought were his enemies. When he recovered, he was overcome with shame, and committed suicide. His ghost refused to speak to Odysseus when the great traveller met him in the Underworld.

With Achilles dead, the Greeks began to wonder if Troy would ever fall. Calchas advised that the city could not be taken without the arrows of Heracles, and Odysseus and Diomedes were despatched to Lemnos to summon Philoctetes, who, cured of his wound, rendered valuable service. His arrows mortally wounded Paris, who struggled back to Troy but died there. The nymph Oenone refused to heal him since he had forsaken her for Helen, but when he died she was overcome with remorse and killed herself.

The death of Paris gave rise to a new rivalry over Helen among the sons of Priam. The king supported the claim of Deiphobus to marry her, and after Helen had been caught trying to escape, she was compelled to become his wife. Many of the Trojans were disgusted, and Helenus, Deiphobus' rival, left the city and went to live on the slopes of Mount Ida.

Top:
The Achaeans emerge from the Trojan Horse. From a black-figure vase painting of the 6th century.

Above:
The fall of Troy: Priam is killed by Neoptolemus (bottom right), and Hector's baby son, last of the Trojan royal line, is hurled from the walls by the Achaean herald. Etruscan vase painting, 4th century B.C.

Helenus knew the secrets that protected Troy, and Agamemnon sent Odysseus to capture him. Helenus revealed that three things were necessary for Troy to fall: the presence of Neoptolemus, son of Achilles; the removal of the Palladium of Athena from the city; and, rather curiously, the presence of the shoulder-blade of Pelops. The latter was sent for from Pisa, and Odysseus with Diomedes and others went to Scyros to fetch the young son of Achilles. Odysseus also entered Troy, disguised as a beggar, and stole, possibly with the aid of Diomedes and, some say, with the connivance of Queen Hecuba, the Palladium, a wooden image of Athena. Certainly there was much dissension in Troy with many, including Aeneas, son of Anchises and representing a junior branch of the royal dynasty, disaffected with the war party.

Odysseus has a dual character. In Homer he is an honourable chieftain, a good warrior, though not the equal of Achilles or Ajax, and immensely clever; almost every cunning stratagem of the Greeks is conceived by him. Other writers make him mean and treacherous, crafty certainly, but untrustworthy and conceited. It is said, for example, that when he and Diomedes had escaped from Troy with the Palladium of Athena, Odysseus tried to kill his old associate in order to gain all the credit for the exploit. Diomedes, forewarned by a flash of moonlight on Odysseus' sword, disarmed him and kicked him all the way back to the ships. Probably, this hostility towards Odysseus by later writers should be discounted.

The device that finally brought about the fall of Troy was probably Odysseus' idea, although it is also said to have been prompted by Athena. A huge, hollow, wooden horse was built, in which Agamemnon, Odysseus himself, and a number of the bravest warriors concealed themselves. The rest of the army burned the camp and put out to sea. To the Trojans it looked as though the Greeks had sailed away at last. One man, Sirion, was left behind. He pretended to have quarrelled with his companions, and told the Trojans that the horse was an offering to Athena, which had deliberately been made too

Menelaus (with shield) recaptures Helen after the fall of Troy. He drew his sword to kill her, but looking at her he softened, and eventually a happy marriage was resumed. From a 5th-century Attic vase painting.

Electra brings a libation to the tomb of her father, Agamemnon, and meets Orestes, previously thought to be dead, with his friend Pylades. Red-figured amphora from Paestum, 4th century.

Above, right:
When Schliemann lifted this gold mask from a dead face at Mycenae, he believed he was looking – for a few seconds before it crumbled – at the face of Agamemnon. In fact, it belongs to the 16th century B.C., some four centuries earlier.

large to pass through the gates of Troy. If it did, the city would become invincible. Not everyone, Laocoön for example, believed this story. But two serpents appeared from the sea and coiled themselves around Laocoön's twin sons. When their father ran to their aid, he too was seized and crushed (this is the subject of what is, after the Venus de Milo, the most famous surviving classical sculpture, now in the Vatican Museum). Priam was thus convinced that Sirion's story was genuine, and the wooden horse was hauled, with some difficulty, into Troy.

There was another voice that accurately forecast ruin, that of Cassandra, daughter of Priam. Apollo, who loved her, had given her the gift of prophecy, but when she rejected his advances he so ordained things that, however accurate her prophecies were, no one would ever believe her.

Under cover of night, while Sirion signalled to the ships waiting out at sea, a trapdoor in the wooden horse opened, and the Greeks descended by a rope-ladder to the ground. Some killed the few sleepy sentries, while others rushed to open the gates and admit the returning army. The battle then, though fierce, was soon over. Priam was killed by Neoptolemus. Deiphobus was killed by Menelaus and Odysseus. Aeneas, carrying his aged father Anchises, escaped; his subsequent adventures belong in a later chapter. The women were all carried off, except Hecuba, who was possibly stoned to death, but later turned into a bitch, some say the sea-monster Scylla. Cassandra was seized by Ajax the Lesser although she was sheltering in Athena's sanctuary. Agamemnon claimed her, but Athena's anger was not easily assuaged. The son of Hector, a baby, was too dangerous to live, and he was thrown from the city walls. His mother, Andromache, became the prize of Neoptolemus. Polyxena, another daughter of

Right:
Odysseus listening to Elpenor, one of his dead comrades, in the Underworld, with Hermes at the right. This brilliantly assured red-figure painting is now in Boston.

Odysseus tied to the mast to resist the songs of the Sirens, one of which is plunging suicidally seawards in mortification at the failure of the lure. This red-figure painting in the British Museum is frequently reproduced as, among other virtues, it gives a uniquely detailed picture of a 5th-century Greek ship (although, like all artists in antiquity, the painter has placed the ship much too high in the water).

Ionian islands.) He who ate the lotus forgot about his home and former existence, and fell into an existence of idle luxury. Odysseus had to use force to get his men back to sea. In the land of the Cyclops, the one-eyed sons of Poseidon, Odysseus and his men went exploring, and entered the cave of Polyphemus to steal food. When the giant returned, he took them prisoner by barring the entrance to the cave with a huge rock. For his supper, Polyphemus ate two of his prisoners, and for breakfast next morning he ate two more. But to escape from the cave presented a tricky problem; it was no good killing the giant, if that were possible, because Odysseus and his dwindling crew were not strong enough to shift the rock that barred the entrance. The strong wine presented by the priest of Apollo put Polyphemus into a deep sleep, and Odysseus then prepared a sharp stake, heated the point, and drove it into the single eye of the Cyclops. The blinded giant awoke roaring with pain and rage. His brother Cyclops, attracted by the noise, asked him from outside the cave what was the matter. Polyphemus made the curious answer, 'No one is killing me', and his brothers went away, thinking he was having a joke or a nightmare. For Odysseus, when Polyphemus had asked him who he was, had told him, 'No one'.

In the morning, Polyphemus was forced to move the rock away from the entrance to let his sheep out to pasture. To make sure that his prisoners did not escape, he passed his hands over each creature as it went out. But Odysseus conceived the clever plan of tying each of his men to the belly of a sheep, and in that way they evaded Polyphemus' touch. When his own turn came to leave, he got past by digging his hands and feet into the fleece of a sheep and hanging on.

Once safely back in his ship, Odysseus could not resist a shouted jeer at Polyphemus, who began hurling enormous rocks in the direction of the sound and nearly sank the ship. Equally dangerous, Polyphemus called on his divine father for vengeance, and from that time on Odysseus, among his other difficulties, had to cope with the hostility of Poseidon, a situation that every navigator ought if possible to avoid.

Odysseus' next host was more hospitable. He was Aeolus, ruler of the winds, and not only did he treat the travellers well, he gave their captain as a leaving present a bag containing the contrary winds. Thus they made good progress, and were nearly home when, while Odysseus was asleep, his men opened the bag in the belief that it contained treasure. The winds rushed out, and the ship was immediately blown back in the direction she had come.

After some unfortunate losses at the hands of the Laestrygones, cannibals of gigantic stature, Odysseus and his surviving crew came to Aeaea, the island of Circe, in the far west. Circe, the sister of Aietes, King of Colchis, was a daughter of the Sun and a powerful enchantress. It was her habit to turn all visitors to her island into animals, and Odysseus' men, whom he sent to explore the island, were promptly changed into pigs when they reached Circe's house and unwisely accepted a drink. Their leader, Eurylochus, had remained outside, and he hurried back to report this disastrous development to his captain. Odysseus, sword in hand, marched angrily towards the palace, but on the way he met Hermes, who gave him an antidote to Circe's magic known only to the gods. Thus, when Circe touched him with her wand and told him to go and join his companions in the pig-sty,

A Roman mosaic of the 3rd century A.D. combines a fishing scene with one of Odysseus and his men passing the Sirens' rock unharmed, thanks to Circe's warning.

135

Odysseus remained unchanged and, brandishing his sword, demanded from Circe a promise of no more tricks and the prompt restoration of his companions. She was so impressed that she at once invited him to be her consort.

Circe bore several sons to Odysseus, but still he was anxious to be gone. She agreed eventually, but suggested he first visit the Underworld to consult the seer, Tiresias, who would tell him how to get home. The Greeks were far from eager to sail to the Underworld, but Odysseus insisted and, thanks to Circe's guidance, he arrived in gloomy Tartaros. He met several old acquaintances there, including his mother, who had died recently. Hearing from Tiresias that his wife, Penelope, was hard-put to resist the crowds of suitors who besieged her, ambitious to take over Odysseus' kingdom, made Odysseus all the more anxious to get back to Ithaca.

After returning to Circe's island, Odysseus set off again, forewarned by the enchantress that the next dangers he would have to pass were the twin menaces of Scylla and Charybdis and the fatal allurement of the Sirens. Odysseus chose to sail closer to Scylla than the fearful whirlpool of Charybdis, thus saving his ship though losing six of his men to the snapping heads of Scylla. There was an alternative course, but that would have meant passing the clashing rocks through which the *Argo* alone had passed in safety. Clearly Odysseus did not know the story that, since the *Argo*'s successful passage, the rocks had become stationary.

The menace of the Sirens was overcome by the plan which Circe had suggested. The Sirens, two or three in number, were bird-like women whose song was irresistible to those who heard it; but the attempt to land on the Sirens' rocks inevitably resulted in shipwreck. Following Circe's advice, Odysseus ordered his men to plug their ears with wax and tie him to the mast—and not to release him no matter how hard he begged. Tied thus to the mast, Odysseus heard the Sirens' song and desperately desired to join them, but his men ignored his pleas and, being deaf, rowed on impervious to the music. The Sirens, seeing their spell fail for the first time, cast themselves into the sea and were drowned.

In—so it is said—Sicily, where Odysseus next stopped, were the pastures where Helios kept his herds of splendid cattle. Odysseus made his men promise not to touch them, but they were hungry and, while he slept, Eurylochus persuaded his fellows to slaughter some of the animals. Helios complained to Zeus, who despatched a thunderbolt that sank the ship. All were drowned except Odysseus himself, who hung on to the mast and, as the wrecked ship was sucked down by Charybdis, seized hold of an olive tree growing out of the cliff above his head. The wreckage was regurgitated by the whirlpool, and Odysseus dropped on to it. For nine days he drifted, and on the tenth he was cast ashore on the island of the nymph Calypso.

The lovely nymph, a daughter of Thetis, greeted Odysseus warmly, and he stayed there for many years, unable to get away. At length Hermes came with a message from Zeus, ordering Calypso to let the wanderer go, and to supply him with a raft and provisions. He set off on his raft of logs, but unfortunately Poseidon noticed him and sent great waves that swamped the raft. He swam for two days, helped by Athena who trespassed on Poseidon's prerogative to subdue the waves. At length he was washed ashore and, crawling to some trees for shelter, he covered himself with leaves and fell asleep.

He was awoken next morning when the princess Nausicaa, daughter of King Alcinous, came down to the beach to play a ball game with her ladies; this is sometimes described as the first recorded ball game in

The bronze mask of some kind of supernatural marine creature, possibly Scylla, now in the British Museum.

Opposite, top:
The return of Odysseus: the traveller was recognised by Eurycleia, the elderly servant who washed his feet. Detail from a red-figured vase painting.

Bottom:
Penelope wasting time at her loom, with Telemachus, her son by Odysseus. Detail from a 5th century skyphos.

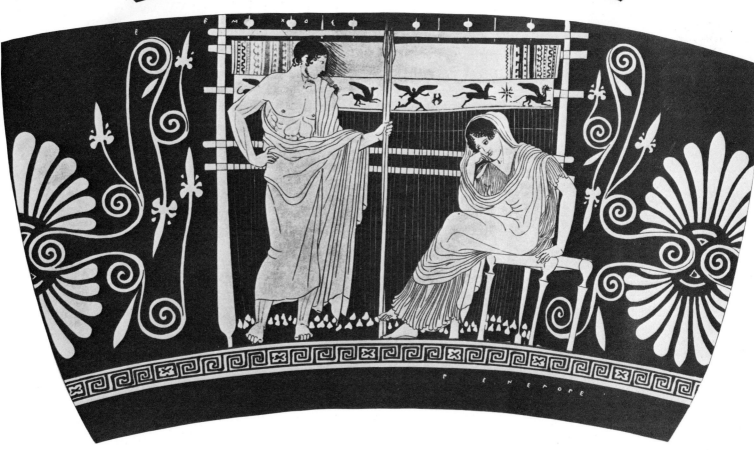

the world. Nausicaa took Odysseus under her protection and, through her intercession, Alcinous provided him with ship and crew to take him to Ithaca. So Odysseus came home, while Alcinous had a great deal of trouble with Poseidon, who resented the help he had given to Odysseus.

When he landed on Ithaca, Odysseus with Athena's help took on the disguise of an old beggar, though as he had been away for something like twenty years it might have been hard to recognize him anyway. He made himself known to his son, Telemachus, and a couple of faithful old retainers, who helped to get him into his own house. Otherwise, no one recognized him except his old dog, Argus, who was lying neglected on a dung heap and just managed to give one wag of his tail before he died. Inside the house, he won the approval of Penelope because he could tell her stories about her husband. She asked Odysseus' old nurse to wash the traveller's feet and, some say, the old lady recognized him by a boyhood scar, but kept silent at Odysseus' prompting.

Penelope, faced with over a hundred importunate suitors who had already made free with Odysseus' property, raped his maids and plotted – unsuccessfully – the death of his son, was almost at her wits' end. She had managed to keep these insolent braggarts at arms' length for a time with the excuse that she must finish a piece of embroidery she was working on before she could take another husband. Each night she would secretly unpick the work she had done that day. But eventually someone saw through this trick and Penelope had to think of another stratagem. The vulgar suitors pressed her to make a choice, and finally she said she would marry the man who could shoot an arrow through twelve rings with Odysseus' old bow. None of them could so much as bend that mighty weapon, until Odysseus himself, who in his guise of beggar had been ill-treated by the suitors, asked if he might try. They jeered, but let him have the bow, and with one smooth action he sent an arrow speeding through the twelve rings. Before his rivals could recover from the shock of recognition – for it was clear that the old beggar was Odysseus himself – he sent a second arrow just as cleanly through the heart of their leader. The rest sprang for their spears, but found they had gone, removed a short time before by Telemachus, who now appeared bearing arms for himself, his father and two faithful retainers. In a bloody fight, these four slew every one of the suitors. Odysseus, after his long absence, claimed his rightful place as King of Ithaca and husband of the faithful Penelope.

There are other versions of the story, and a variety of subsequent adventures are ascribed to Odysseus. But the most satisfactory place to leave the great wanderer is in triumph at Ithaca, where Homer left him at the end of the *Odyssey*.

Odysseus shoots down the greedy suitors, one of whom uses a table as a shield against the arrows. From an Attic vase painting in the Berlin Museum.

Lesser Gods and Spirits

The powerful anthropomorphizing urge of the Greeks turned the sun itself into a distinctly human creature. Helios was the son of two of the Titans, Hyperion and Thea. Although he is 'all-seeing', he was seldom a subject of divine worship, and his numerous appearances in myth are almost all little more than walk-on parts. As a rule he drives a four-horse chariot, sometimes rides a horse, and he lives in the east, beyond the dawn. After driving across the sky, he descends each evening into the ocean, or into Ocean, which surrounds Earth, and in the course of the night he is carried gently back to his home in the East. In late writings he is sometimes identified with Apollo.

The chief appearances in myth of Helios have been mentioned in the foregoing chapters: his warning to Hephaestus about Aphrodite and Ares, and the theft of some of his cattle by the companions of Odysseus. He had various love affairs and several formidable children. Aietes and Circe were his children by Perseis. Another son was Phaeton, who was eager to drive his father's chariot and impress his sisters. At last Helios allowed him to do so, but he could not control the horses and drove first too high, so that Earth froze, then too low, so it was scorched. Zeus, in a rage, threw a thunderbolt that killed him, and he fell into a river. His grieving sisters were turned into trees and their tears became the gum of amber.

The mother of these children was Rhode, and the island of Rhodes was the chief centre of the worship of Helios. When Zeus was sharing out the places on earth to the gods and goddesses, he had just come to the end of the list when he realized he had left out Helios. He was about to begin all over again, but Helios indicated a new island just rising from the sea which he said would satisfy him. Sicily, which developed from a fallen missile in the battle between the Olympians and the Giants, was later added to the dominions of Helios. It was another of his sons by Rhode, so the Greeks said, who having killed one of his brothers fled to Egypt and founded the city of Heliopolis.

Selene, the moon, was the sister of Helios. Later, she was sometimes called his daughter, and later still she was identified with Artemis, as Helios was identified with the brother of Artemis. Selene drives a chariot, but it is not a quadriga like her brother's, being drawn by only a pair, some say a pair of white oxen. From a strictly mythological point of view, she is of little importance. She is said to have been the mother, probably by Zeus, of the Nemean lion, one of the monsters killed by Heracles, and she does feature in one well-known story, that of Endymion.

Endymion, a great hunter, was a son of Zeus by the nymph Calyce. Selene fell in love with him when she saw him lying asleep, and as a result of the ensuing affair Endymion now lies in perpetual sleep,

Helios, the Sun, driving his chariot across the sky. For some reason the quadriga (four horses in line) has always been regarded as the grandest type of horse carriage, although it is actually very inefficient, as the inside horses tend to do all the work.

never ageing, though there are several explanations of how this came about. One story is that, having borne fifty children to him, Selene decided she preferred him as she had first seen him, when she had gently kissed his eyelids without his awakening. Another says that Endymion made advances to Hera, and Zeus put him to sleep for ever. A third says that Endymion sleeps perpetually by his own wish, as he could not face the prospect of growing old.

The Titans Hyperion and Thea had a third sibling, Eos, the dawn, described by poets from Homer down as 'rosy-fingered'. She also drives a chariot. She is a more substantial personality than Selene, and figures in a love story which presents a kind of alternative to the myth of Endymion.

Eos fell in love with Tithonus and carried him off. Some say she carried off at the same time another beautiful boy, Ganymede, whom Zeus appropriated. Eos asked Zeus to make Tithonus immortal, but she forgot to ask also for the gift of perpetual youth. Zeus granted her request, but as the years went by Tithonus became older and greyer and more shrunken. Finally, Eos closed the door on him, and he turned into a cicada.

Eos had a number of interesting lovers, including Orion, whom she fell in love with while he was blind, and Cleitus, a grandson of Melampus. By Cephalus she had a son, Phaethon, who was carried off by Aphrodite. It was this Cephalus who, in later writings, was the husband of the unfortunate Procris; he killed her accidentally, thinking she was a deer, with his spear that never missed.

Of all the deities, none changed so drastically in character as Eros, the god of sexual desire. We know him best in a very late characterisation as a larking child who shoots his arrows of romantic love in an arbitrary and irresponsible manner. He is regarded as the son of Aphrodite. But in earlier writings he was merely the attendant of Aphrodite, and earlier still he was one of the oldest of the gods. He was particularly associated with youth and homosexual desire.

The only well-known story in which he appears is a very late tale from a time when Eros had turned into Cupid. It is hardly to be classed as a myth, but as H. J. Rose said, 'it is the only folk-tale told as such by any classical writer' (i.e. Apuleius), and worth repeating.

Psyche was a princess who was so beautiful that she made Venus (Aphrodite) jealous, and the goddess sent Cupid to make her fall in love with someone thoroughly unsuitable. But when Cupid saw her, he fell in love with her himself, and contrived to have her moved to some distant palace where he might visit her stealthily. Psyche was happy with this arrangement although she was not allowed to see her husband; but she was lonely and asked for her sisters to visit her. This was permitted, but her sisters were jealous creatures. They told Psyche that her husband was a man-eating monster, and gave her a lamp and a knife to kill him. Next time Cupid visited her, Psyche lit the lamp, and was overcome by the beauty of the god. But a drop of oil from the lamp awakened him. He was angry at her disobedience, and left her. Psyche set out to look for him, and eventually came to the house of Venus, who treated her badly, set her unpleasant tasks to do, and finally put her into a perpetual sleep. From that state she was rescued by Cupid, who had persuaded Jupiter (Zeus) to let him marry a mortal, and the two lived happily ever after.

Asklepios, the god of medicine, called by the Romans Aesculapius, was the son of Apollo—fittingly, as Apollo himself was connected with healing. Apollo loved Coronis but she, although pregnant by Apollo, slept with a mortal, Ischys, and Apollo found out, warned, it is said, by the crow, which he thereupon changed from white to black

These figures engraved on a bronze Etruscan mirror back are believed to be Eos, the Dawn, and her reluctant lover, Cephalus.

Below:
In this scene in relief on a Roman sarcophagus, Selene, the Moon, spots the sleeping Endymion and, guided by a satyr, alights from her chariot (only two horses, unlike the grander Sun) to investigate more closely.

(Athena is also said to be responsible for the black plumage of the once white crow). Artemis inflicted vengeance on behalf of her brother and killed Coronis with her arrows. As the body was about to burn on the funeral pyre, Apollo remembered that Coronis had been pregnant and told Hermes to cut the child from the body. He did so, and it was a boy, Asklepios. The child was reared by the wise Centaur, Chiron, and learned from him the arts of medicine. Apollo also assisted in his education, and so did Athena, who gave him some of the Gorgon's blood. The blood from the left side of the Gorgon would raise the dead to life; that from the right side would kill instantly.

Asklepios had a number of children, some of them vaguely personi-fied concepts such as Hygieia and Panacea, others totally human figures like the surgeons with the Greek army at the siege of Troy. The status of Asklepios himself—god or hero?—is a matter of argu-ment: in Homer he is a mortal, and his fate at the hands of Zeus suggests that he may have been a hero who was later deified rather than a god from the first.

Hygeia, daughter of Asklepios (he had another daughter, Panacea). Statue from Epidaurus.

Above, right:
The porch of the Asklepeion at Pergamon. The mountain city was one of the great healing centres of antiquity.

For Asklepios' habit of raising the dead caused trouble. It seemed to infringe on divine authority and, in particular, it annoyed Hades, who resented his acquisitions being whisked away again. It is said that the case of Hippolytus, whom Asklepios restored to life at the request of Artemis, for a large fee paid in gold, was decisive. Zeus hurled a thunderbolt, and Asklepios himself descended to the Underworld.

Apollo was furious, and though he could do nothing against his mighty father, he took some revenge by killing the Cyclops, who had made the thunderbolt. It was for this murder that he served a year as herdsman to Admetus. Later writers say that Asklepios was himself restored to life. Asklepios' symbol is the snake, which is 'reborn' when it sheds its skin.

Pan was a very old god indeed, much older, probably, then Hermes, who is usually described as his father, though there are many other candidates for this honour, including Zeus. Hermes at least came from Arcadia, which was the home of Pan also. The story that Pan's mother was Penelope seems most unlikely. He is the god of herds, especially goats, and is himself usually goat-like in form: his goatishness also reflects his lecherous nature. Though generally easy-going in nature, he was angry if awoken from his siesta, and he had the curious power of inducing an unreasonable terror in people in isolated situations; this emotion is called after him – panic. (Pan's own name is derived from a word meaning 'pasture', rather than 'all-embracing' as in Pan-American or Pan-African.)

Pan's amorous conquests were many, though perhaps not as numerous as he claimed: he said he had slept with every one of the Maenads. His most famous conquest was Selene. He lured her into the woods with a beautiful white fleece, which covered his own black hairiness and concealed his identity from Selene, who certainly seems to be out of place in such gross company. Pan strongly suggests a not un-common human type–the inveterate womanizer of grossly unattractive appearance whose conquests belie his looks–but his love for a succession of nymphs was usually unrequited. His connection with pine trees is explained by one of these failures, for the nymph Pitys was turned into a pine tree while fleeing from the lustful Pan. Another of Pan's attributes—his musicianship—is linked with the nymph Syrinx, who similarly evaded Pan by metamorphosis, turning into a bank of reeds. Pan cut the reeds, and from them he fashioned his pipes. These, it is said, were the first pipes, and those that Hermes claimed to have invented, and sold to Apollo in exchange for Apollo's cattle, were copied from the original pan-pipes. It was from Pan also that Apollo learned the art of prophecy.

A third nymph loved by Pan was Echo who, according to one story, was torn to pieces by shepherds driven mad by Pan when he found he could not capture her. Only her voice remained. But it is also said that Echo had a child by Pan, and her fate is differently explained: Echo offended Hera by distracting her so that Zeus could carry on his extra-marital affairs without the interference of his wife, and for this Hera deprived her of the power of speech, except to repeat the last words of the previous speaker. Subsequently, she fell in love with the beautiful Narcissus, but that self-centred young man would have nothing to do with her and she wasted away out of grief until only her voice remained. Retribution fell upon Narcissus, for as he bent down to drink from a spring he saw his face reflected in the water and promptly fell in love with himself. So enamoured was he by his own image that he remained gazing into the water until he too wasted away. Then he was turned into a flower. Others say that Narcissus was punished by Artemis for rejecting another suitor, who killed himself, calling on the gods for revenge. Narcissus stabbed himself by the spring, and the narcissus grew from his blood.

Another beautiful youth cut off in his prime, who was associated with Pan, was Daphnis. The name is most familiar in conjunction with that of Chloe, but that was a pastoral romance of about the 2nd century A.D. and has nothing to do with the mythological Daphnis. He was a Sicilian herdsman and the friend of Pan, perhaps his brother,

The Nereids (sea nymphs) as the Romans saw them, with strange sea creatures frisking around them. Mosaic of the 3rd century A.D.

145

An epicene Narcissus gazing
adoringly at his own image.
From a Pompeian mural.

for Hermes is said to have been his father and one of the nymphs his
mother. Pan taught him to play the pipes and Artemis took him hunting. He was blinded by a nymph to whom he had been unfaithful, and
thereafter composed sad songs about his fate. These were the first
shepherds' songs. But Daphnis did not live long, being carried off by
Hermes, who caused a spring to gush from the spot where he disappeared.

Although Pan remained a minor god, and was somewhat roughly
treated by Arcadian hunters who gave his image a beating if they killed
no game, he nevertheless acquired a certain respect throughout the
Greek world. He had a cult at Athens which dated from the time of the
battle of Marathon, when Pan waylaid an Athenian herald to inquire
why the Athenians ignored him, since he had helped them. A shrine
was built below the Acropolis, and an annual ceremony, with a torch
race and sacrifices, was held in his honour.

According to one strange story, however, Pan is dead – the only
god to have died. As told by Plutarch, an Italian ship bound for
Greece heard a message shouted from an island which said 'the great
Pan is dead'. It addressed the pilot of the ship, Thamus, by name, and
he passed the message on to the mainland, where it was received with
lamentation. The explanation usually given for this curious story is
that the original message was misheard: Thamus, who was an
Egyptian, shared the name of the man whose death was being announced and thought the adjective 'all-great', applied to the dead
Thamus, referred to the god Pan.

Pan is sometimes associated with Dionysus, whose donkey he
killed after he had defeated it in argument, and they are both frequently attended by woodland spirits, nymphs and satyrs. The

A Greek marble of the 6th
century B.C. showing a herdsman
carrying a calf. Apollo, Hermes
and Pan were all pastoral deities –
Pan was probably the most
ancient, and never lost his
following in spite of his more
glamorous rivals.

Below :
The mountains of Arcadia. This
was the home of Pan: the lower
slopes were intensively used by
shepherds and goatherds from
earliest times.

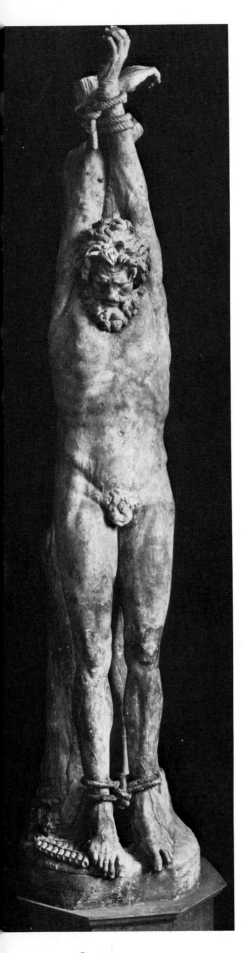

nymphs are—usually—amorous maidens of the trees (Driads and Hamadriads) and of the water (Naiads and Nereids). One or two of them acquired definite personalities and became goddesses of at least local importance, but on the whole they are merely incidental attendants involved in various rustic cults. They are half-way between gods and mortals, being very long-lived but not immortal. Some of the tree nymphs were thought to die when their individual trees were cut down.

The satyrs were originally undifferentiated woodland spirits, the brothers of the nymphs. As associates of Pan, they are often horned and goat-footed, as in the famous sculpture after Praxiteles of a satyr playing a flute, though they also appear as riotous but good-looking young men. They acquired a considerable reputation for lechery, and in later times became the symbols of male sexuality. They were dangerous when under the influence of the Dionysiac frenzy, but were otherwise rather cowardly. They seldom appear as individuals; Marsyas is an exception, as the challenger of Apollo.

The older satyrs were called Sileni; though sometimes Silenus is an individual. They are wiser as well as older, but they drink even more and often appear in art semi-conscious from the effects of wine. There was a stone in Athens on which Silenus had sat when he came to the city with Dionysus, and Pausanias, the geographer who wrote a *Description of Greece* in the 2nd century A.D., found a temple dedicated to Silenus at Elis. Silenus, or the Sileni, appear to have taken a pessimistic view of human existence. When captured by King Midas, who laced a local spring to make him drunk, Silenus told the king that it were best for a man never to be born, but if he were, then he should hope to die as soon as possible.

Midas himself was not a god or spirit but 'a kind of king of Fairyland' in Greek folklore. He was the richest and most avaricious man in the world and possessed some beautiful rose gardens, in which Silenus was captured. Having fed him well and sent him back to Dionysus, Midas was granted fulfilment of his dearest wish. Like many another character in folklore, Midas forgot to allow for the precision with which such wishes were granted. He asked that everything he touched might turn to gold, and so it did. Even the food turned to gold when he tried to eat it, and he had to ask for his gift to be removed. He was ordered to wash in the sands of the river Pactolus: his gift disappeared, but the sands have been gold ever since.

It will be remembered that Midas was one of the judges in the music contest between Apollo and Marsyas—in some versions between Apollo and Pan—and, unwisely voting for the latter, was given donkey's ears by Apollo as a comment on his musical taste. Midas in shame hid his ears under a Phrygian cap (Phrygia is usually identified as his kingdom; he succeeded Gordius, the fastener of the Gordian knot that no one could undo until Alexander pulled out the stake to which it was fastened). Only his barber knew the secret that Midas concealed under his cap, and he was solemnly charged to keep silent. But after a while, the barber found the compulsion to tell too hard to resist, so he went and whispered the secret into a hole in the ground. Unfortunately, reeds sprouted from the hole, and whenever the wind moved them, they whispered, 'King Midas has asses' ears'.

There were a number of other rustic gods in Greece. Priapus has already made a brief entrance. His hideous, dwarfish appearance and obscenely large genitals are explained as the result of Hera's curse, inflicted because of her disapproval of the behaviour of his mother, Aphrodite. His father was sometimes said to be Dionysus, sometimes the beautiful youth Adonis. His image was often placed at entrances as a good-luck charm, and he may be regarded as the original garden

gnome. In some places he was worshipped as a fertility god, and perhaps identified with Eros. He once tried to make surreptitious love to Hestia, but she was awoken by the bray of a donkey (an animal identified with lust and thus often associated with Priapus), gave a scream, and sent Priapus fleeing in fright.

Another rather obscure minor god of the countryside was Aristaeus. He is best remembered, if he is remembered at all, as the father of Actaeon, who was turned into a stag by Artemis and killed by his own hounds. The wife of Aristaeus was Autonoe, one of the daughters of Cadmus, and his mother was Cyrene, a Thessalian girl of Amazonian inclinations, later numbered among the Naiads, who caught the eye of Apollo by the elegance with which she fought a lion. Aristaeus was the eventual result. He is the god of olive-growing, bee-keeping, and cheese-making.

Advised by the oracle of Delphi, Aristaeus went to the island of Ceos, where he was instrumental in relieving the people of a plague, and Zeus, as a mark of commendation, sent the Etesian winds which cool all Greece for forty days in the summer. Some time later, Aristaeus suffered himself from a plague which killed all his bees. He learned from Proteus, the herdsman of the sea, that this curse had been placed upon him by the Dryads. They were angry with him because he had caused the death of Eurydice, who sustained her fatal snake bite while evading his amorous pursuit. Thus advised, Aristaeus prepared a generous sacrifice to the Dryads, slaughtering a number of cattle. His mother, Cyrene, told him to leave the carcasses of the animals where they lay, and after nine days a swarm of bees rose from

A Roman marble figure of Silenus, now in the Vatican Museum. Silenus was sometimes a single character, sometimes one of a band of satyr-like creatures – Sileni – who were followers of Dionysus.

them and settled in a tree, where Aristaeus caught them. (Bees were commonly connected with the bodies of a dead animal, usually a lion, in mythology; such a story occurs in the Old Testament: *Judges* XV, 8.)

Aristaeus was a considerable traveller, and is associated with many widely separated places. He departed from Boeotia after the death of Actaeon and visited North Africa before settling for some time in Sardinia, where he was joined by Daedalus. He resided for some years among the olive-growers of Sicily, and was said to be one of the followers of Dionysus in Thrace.

Aristaeus and his son Actaeon have some similarities to Orion. Two other figures somewhat in this mould were Otus and Ephialtes. They were twin sons of Poseidon and their mother was Iphimedia, a mortal. According to Odysseus, who saw them in the Underworld, they were the tallest men earth had produced, finer than all but Orion. Before their ninth birthday they were nine cubits across the shoulders and nine fathoms high. Their rowdy ambitions disturbed the gods, for they planned to build a staircase up to Heaven by piling one mountain on top of another. They captured Ares and put him in a bronze pot, from which Hermes had to rescue him, and they planned to seize Hera and Artemis for themselves. Such presumption, needless to say, did not long go unpunished. Some say Apollo killed them, others that Artemis made them kill themselves by sending a deer between them at which they fired an arrow simultaneously, missing the deer and hitting each other. This fulfilled a prophecy that the brothers could be killed neither by gods nor men. A later writer says that in Tartaros they were bound back to back with live snakes, but Odysseus, i.e. Homer, did not mention that detail.

Other legends, however, portray Otus and Ephialtes in quite a different light, not as oversized juvenile delinquents but as minor gods of benign influence. They are associated particularly with the island of Naxos, and their mother Iphimedia may have been a personification of the Earth-mother. They are called the Aloedi, 'children of the threshing floor'.

The Gods of Rome

The mythology of the Greeks was extremely popular in ancient times, and was exported all over the Mediterranean world and beyond. Greek writers freely supplied myths for other peoples, borrowing most of the raw material from their own rich heritage. There are even Greek versions of perfectly adequate and well-recorded myths of the Egyptians and the Jews, sometimes bearing little relationship to the original, genuine myth. The mythology of Egypt and Judaea has survived because it was written down, just as the Greeks wrote down their own legends; but this was not the case in Italy. In that much younger society, Greek influence was strong–almost overwhelming– before Italian traditions could be permanently recorded. Moreover, at a later date, the Romans deliberately and wholeheartedly adopted the Greek myths as their own, assimilating their own gods to Greek ones and manufacturing new 'myths', largely for political reasons, on Greek models. It was commonly believed in the Ancient World that the gods worshipped by other peoples must be the same gods under different names. Thus, the traditions current in republican Rome were not, for the most part, genuine Italian traditions. Many of them are clearly of recent manufacture, or are based on foreign, chiefly Greek legends. Of course, the early Latins must have had, like every other people, imaginative stories and traditions of their own; but they have not been preserved. Here and there, fragments have survived, though some of these may be based on Greek sources of which we are also ignorant; but modern scholarship tends to show that the authentically Italian content of Roman mythology is unfortunately rather small.

The first people in Italy who could write (though their writing has not yet been fully deciphered) were the Etruscans. They were the last and the most advanced of a series of invaders, and they came, probably, from Asia Minor in the 9th century B.C., settling in Etruria. At the height of their power they briefly controlled an area which stretched from the Po valley in the north to Naples in the south. The site of Rome was partly determined by the need for defence against the Etruscans in the north: the Latins, the less-advanced people who founded Rome, decided they could fortify the hills on the Tiber where Rome now stands.

The Etruscans were able potters and builders, masters of bronze, who in their art strikingly combined naturalism and convention. They gave particular attention to their tombs, and, from what we know of it, their religion was decidedly grim; it included an important cult of the dead. They had great influence on the early development of Rome, and provided some of its legendary early kings.

This famous Etruscan bronze she-wolf dates from the 5th century B.C. The figures of Romulus and Remus look like a pair of Renaissance *putti*—and that is exactly what they are, having been added to the original about 2,000 years later.

Tina, the Etruscan fire god (right) who, like Zeus, carried a thunderbolt in his hand. He spoke in the thunder and rode to earth on a flash of lightning. On the left is Una, the Etruscan goddess who corresponds to Juno, though her association with the sex life of women suggests a moon-goddess connotation. Bronzes, in the Fitzwilliam Museum, Cambridge.

As Italian tourist agencies are keen to remind us, there are more classical Greek remains in Italy than there are in Greece herself. Greek colonists had started settling in southern Italy—in what became known as *Magna Graecia*—in the 8th century B.C. They were probably present even before Rome was founded (the date traditionally given is 753 B.C.). Certainly Greek influence was considerable long before that, going back to Mycenaean times. As the Etruscans also were heavily influenced by the Greeks, from whom they may have learned the art of writing, and as the Romans became almost slavish admirers of Greek culture (their opinion of the Greeks as practical people was very different), the Greek influence on Roman civilization was enormous.

In view of the later assimilation of Greek gods, it is important to recognize that the early gods of the Romans were entirely different. The Greek gods were thorough individuals, with characters as complete as any historical persons, showing all the human emotions as well as divine powers. The Roman gods did not, originally, have human personalities, and thus had no myths attached to them. In a way they were no more real than the supernatural forces associated with natural phenomena—rivers, mountains, trees and so on. The 1st century B.C. historian, Varro, believed that in the early days the gods of Rome were worshipped without images. The stories that treat the gods as man-like individuals, if not Greek, are merely the elegant tales of writers like Ovid, mentally far removed from early Roman religious belief. The Roman gods had clearly defined functions—Mars was the god of war, Vulcan the god of fire—but they did not have wives and families, amorous escapades, fits of jealousy, or any of the other attributes of the Olympian family.

Jupiter, the chief Roman god, was in origin a rather insignificant deity, perhaps nothing more than a stone, dating from a time before the use of metals when all useful objects were made of stone. Jupiter was, like Zeus, a sky god, or god of light, and was associated with

Dionysus (Bacchus) and two satyrs, from an Etruscan bronze urn lid.

153

The Forum in morning light, showing the three surviving columns of the temple of Castor and Pollux. The semi-divine twins were popular with the Romans, who believed the twins had fought on the Roman side at the Battle of Lake Regillus.

Below:
An Etruscan representation of Apollo, which suggests a formidable, rather sinister god. As a Roman deity his original powers were those of a god of healing; acknowledgment of his oracular powers coming later. The Sibyl of Cumae was his priestess, fulfilling the same function as the Pythoness of Delphi.

Below, right:
Minerva, the Roman equivalent of Athene, went to Rome from the Etruscans. Her attributes as a champion of the state were mixed with those of an ancient Italian goddess of handicrafts and she was patroness of artisans as well as a goddess of war.

154

the weather, especially thunderstorms. He was the protector of the Latin race and of the family. Juno, his consort, the protector of women, was associated particularly with marriage and child-bearing. She was originally a Moon goddess.

After Jupiter, the most important Roman god was Mars, whose name was given to the first month of the Roman year, which was also the beginning of the campaigning season. The spears of Mars, which were also identified with the god himself, were shaken by the consul on the outbreak of war in order to rouse him from sleep. But Mars had other attributes. He was connected with farming, and protected the crops against damage. The growing season of course coincided with the campaigning season, so his concerns were not so disparate as they may appear.

Vulcan was a fire god, but of an ominous kind, for he was associated with dangerous fires, and his shrines were usually built outside city walls. Originally, he had none of the craftsmanlike attributes of Hephaestus, though he naturally acquired them when he became identified with the Greek smith god. Similarly, Minerva was not originally akin to Athena, whose character she later adopted. Among the Etruscans, she formed a kind of trinity with Jupiter and Juno, and was associated with domestic crafts. Her artistic and intellectual interests – drama, education, etc. – were acquired later. A very late story (obviously late since it treats the deities as humanized individuals) tells how Mars once wished to marry Minerva. He used the goddess of the year, Anna, ugly and elderly, as go-between, but she tricked him, for when he raised the bridal veil after the wedding ceremony he found beneath it not the beautiful countenance of Minerva, but the complacently smirking face of the hideous old Anna.

Jupiter, holding thunderbolts and, in his left hand, a staff surmounted by the Roman eagle. A Roman assimilation of Zeus, as far as religious worship was concerned he figured less prominently than Mars.

Above, left:
Mars, the most Roman of gods and, after Jupiter, the most formidable: the god of the most important activities in Roman life, farming and fighting. Tradition made him also the father of Romulus, and thus of Rome. Marble statue in the Capitoline Museum.

Ovid, incidentally, explains Mars' miraculous birth to Juno, with the aid only of a sacred flower provided by Flora, goddess of blossoms, as Juno's counter-stroke to the birth of Athena.

A god who, like Mars, seems to have been distinctively Roman was the two-headed god Janus, whose image is familiar from coins. He was, however, no more substantial than other Roman gods. He was the god of gates, originally one particular gate – the Janus gate, which was identified with the god. From there he came to preside over all the gates and doorways of the city. Because he was the god of beginnings, his name was listed first, ahead of Jupiter. Ovid tells one of his amusing tales about the two-faced Janus. There was a certain nymph who encouraged amorous advances but made each hopeful suitor precede her into her cave. While his back was turned she ran away. With Janus, naturally, this scheme did not work, and she was compelled to go through with the affair. He was so grateful that he granted her power over the Striges, nasty, harpy-like creatures of the night.

A mosaic in Hadrian's villa depicting one of the Pales (they could be male or female), the ancient spirits of the earth. Their festival was the Parilia, on 21 April, when flocks were ritually purified and prayers offered for a prosperous season.

Left:
Venus was originally, in Roman religion, the spirit of gardens. Later she became identified with Aphrodite and was thus, as the mother of Aeneas, particularly revered as Venus *Genetrix*. Detail from a Pompeian fresco.

Juno Regina, queen of the gods. Originally an ancient Italian goddess of light, she had many aspects in Roman times, mostly concerned with marriage and childbirth. She lifted the curse of sterility which afflicted the Sabine women after their abduction. Marble statue in the Vatican Museum.

Above, right:
Juno Sospita, the protector of women in labour, who became also the liberator. A small statue from Lanuvium, where her temple was guarded by a snake to whom an alleged virgin would offer cake in a ceremony that proved – if the snake ate the cake – that she was indeed a virgin.

Akin to Janus was Terminus, god of boundaries, who was a stone, sanctified by ritual, marking the division between estates.

Another agricultural god was Saturn, who later became identified, rather oddly, with Cronus. He was associated particularly with seed-sowing, and his name may derive from a word meaning 'sower'. He seems to have been linked at one time with an obscure fire goddess, later with Rhea. His festival, the Saturnalia, took place in December, perhaps when the winter grain crop was sown. It lasted seven days, and no public business of any kind was conducted during that week. Slaves were temporarily granted freedom and general license prevailed. Similar customs are quite common in other societies, and linger on in the convention followed by many military bodies in which Christmas dinner is served to the men by the officers and the obligations of rank are lifted.

Vesta, the Roman goddess of the hearth and the counterpart of the Greek Hestia – a case where the names are virtually identical – was very important to the Romans, much more than Hestia was to the Greeks. In early Rome, the constant maintenance of a fire was a vital duty, for which the daughters of the king were responsible. In later times that function was performed by the Vestal Virgins, originally only two in number but later six, who also performed the rituals of worship at the shrine. They were subject to severe discipline at the hands of the Pontifex Maximus, who fulfilled the role of the early kings, and they could be buried alive if they broke their vows of chastity.

The convent-like house of the Vestal Virgins must have been an extremely boring place to live, and there are hints in historic times of restlessness with their lot among the younger Vestals. Their servitude was not permanent, but by the time they were released they were middle-aged and seldom took husbands, which they were then allowed to do. However, they also enjoyed great prestige and several were commemorated in sculpture. Certain legends were also told about them. For example, Aemilia was held responsible for letting the fire go out, for which the usual penalty was a whipping from the

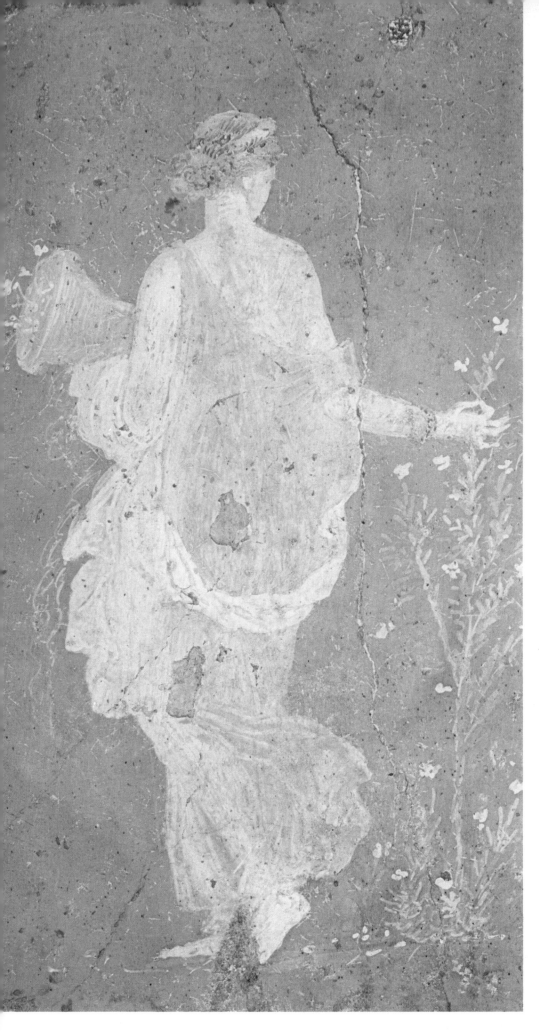

Left :
Flora. The Roman goddess of
flowering plants as depicted in a
fresco from Stabia.

Below :
The god of agriculture in Roman
religion (the sower), Saturn was
probably a version of the Greek
Cronus and reached Rome by
way of the Etruscans. (Cronus,
apart from being the father of
Zeus, was a corn god in very
ancient times). Statuette of the
3rd century A.D.

The Vestal Virgins attending the goddess, who would have appeared on the right. Their importance in Rome reflected the beginnings of Roman religion as a family matter. Relief in the Archaeological Museum, Palermo.

Above:
The two-faced god Janus, on a Roman coin. Originally probably a sun-god, he was, it would seem, exclusively Roman.

Below:
Vesta, the goddess of the hearth, appears here as the tutelary goddess of the bakers' guild. Marble relief in the State Museum, Berlin.

Pontifex Maximus. She called on Vesta to prove her innocence of sacrilege and flung a strip of her garment on the dead fire, which at once burst into flame. Another Vestal proved her chastity by carrying water in a sieve.

The temple of Vesta in the Forum was a circular building, always rebuilt in the same shape on the occasions, surprisingly frequent, when it was destroyed by fire. No doubt it symbolized the original round mud huts of the rude Latins, though Plutarch advanced a more sophisticated explanation – that it represented the universe with the ever-burning fire as the sun. As in all sacred shrines, a tabu prevented laymen entering the premises, and when the consul Metellus did so in 214 B.C., for the honourable purpose of saving sacred objects from destruction, he was struck blind for the sacrilege.

Besides the comparatively well-known deities of Rome, there were many, many more – an innumerable number in fact. For every situation, every event however insignificant, every conceivable activity, there was some minor god or other. They were all very vague, so much so that their worshippers were often uncertain whether they were worshipping a god or a goddess.

There is nothing very strange in that in view of the fact that the Romans did not anthropomorphize their gods as the Greeks did. That they failed to do so does not mean that the Romans were less religious than the Greeks. Some people would argue, on the contrary, that the Roman idea of *numen* was spiritually a finer conception than the humanized deities of Greece. *Numen* implies vitality, and could be possessed by what we would describe as inanimate objects – such as boundary stones. What the early Romans really worshipped were not gods in the Greek sense, but *numina*, spiritual vitalities performing very specific functions. Thus the entrance to a temple, for example, was guarded by three *numina* – the threshold, the door, and the hinge of the door. These countless *numina* had names and functions, but nothing much else. Spinensis, for example, helped farmers clear their fields of thorns; Cloacina, later absorbed by Venus (Aphrodite), looked after the drains.

Much of the ritual involved in the worship or propitiation of such deities was nearer to magic than religion. For example, it was important that rituals were performed with complete precision. If any little detail went wrong, the whole performance had to begin again, which could be expensive if it involved the sacrifice of valuable animals. But otherwise, the spell would not work. In certain instances the equivalent of a safety clause was inserted: an extra sacrifice offered in atonement for any error knowingly or unknowingly committed in the ceremony proper. The actual words pronounced by the priests were not to be audible to the generality, and a clamorous musical background drowned out any other sounds, whose intrusion would be a bad omen. This is but magic–practical magic, concerned exclusively with ensuring material well-being in one way or another–but magic all the same. In early Roman law the casting of spells – witchcraft – was expressly forbidden. Horace recalls the story of the horrid witch Canidia, who made up her evil potions from bits of human bodies which she dug up at night, and once buried a child up to his neck until he starved to death in order to obtain some vital ingredient.

The Suovetaurilia, the sacrificial rite which ensured a good harvest, beneficial weather and fertility in the herds. An augur stands by the altar on the left while the first victim, a bull, is followed by the second, a ram. A boar, not seen in this section of an altar frieze of the 1st century B.C., would have come third.

Venus is not normally associated with sewers, but one of her aspects in Rome was nonetheless Venus Cloacina, the goddess of drains. However, the Roman sewers were major structures of which the citizens were rightly proud. Their outlets can still be seen, as in this photograph.

161

Founders, Kings and Heroes

The messenger god Mercury, who reminded Aeneas that he should not linger with Dido in Carthage but get on with his divinely appointed task of founding a new race in Italy. A marble statue in the Vatican Museum.

In the *Iliad* of Homer, Aeneas, one of the princes of Troy, escapes from the captured city with the aid of Poseidon, who forecasts that Aeneas and his descendants will be great rulers, though he does not say where. A later tradition had him sailing to Italy and founding the city of Rome; the earliest-known source for this legend in complete form comes from the 3rd century B.C. For several reasons, the Romans found the legend satisfying. They wished to establish a direct link with the admired cultural world of Greece, and to fit their own origins into the Greek epics. But the Greeks had been their enemies: Pyrrhus, their chief opponent in the 3rd century B.C., claimed descent from Achilles, and in the Trojan War the Romans felt themselves to be the natural allies of Troy. A Trojan hero therefore made an ideal founder of Rome. Moreover, the tale of Aeneas escaping from the city with his elderly father and household gods appealed to the Roman sense of piety and the cult of the hearth. The idea of Aeneas as the founder of Rome, and of other Trojan heroes as founders of other Italian cities, became generally accepted; but it was not until the greatest poet of classical Rome, Virgil, made Aeneas the central figure in his last and perhaps finest work, a national epic justifying the imperial regime, that the capacity of the legend was fully realized.

'I sing of arms', the *Aeneid* famously begins, and of the man who, driven from Troy and knocked about by the wrath of Juno, finally brought his gods to Latium and fathered the people who built Rome.

Driven by storms, Aeneas arrived in North Africa. Three of his ships were sunk by Juno, enemy of the Trojans, but Neptune (Poseidon) calmed the sea to prevent further disasters. Journeying inland, Aeneas came to the city of Carthage, a city loved by Juno above all others. On the way he met what appeared to be a Spartan maid but turned out to be Venus – the mother of Aeneas – who gave him some useful hints about the immediate future. Venus was also responsible for making the queen of Carthage, Dido, fall in love with Aeneas. The goddess then retired to her home at Paphos, where stood her temple 'warm with incense-smoke and sweet with fresh-plucked blossoms'.

Well-entertained by Dido at Carthage, Aeneas related his earlier adventures. He had first visited Thrace, then Delos, where the oracle told him to visit the land of his ancestors. This he took to mean Crete, as the ancestor of the Trojan royal house came from there, but a plague broke out in Crete, and Aeneas was told by his household gods that his true ancestral home was in Italy. After surviving an attack by the Harpies, he came to Epirus where the king was Helenus, the son of Priam who had told the Greeks why the city could not be captured; he was then married to Andromache, Neoptolemus having

died. The advice of Helenus was to consult the Sibyl at Cumae (the most influential centre of Greek culture in Italy), so he travelled to western Sicily, avoiding the Cyclops on the way, where he was well received by a relation, Acestes, at whose court his father, old Anchises, died. On the way to Cumae, the storm sent by Juno had driven him to Africa.

By the time Aeneas had finished his story, which takes up two of the twelve books of the *Aeneid*, Dido, in spite of her pledge that she would never marry again after the murder of her first husband in her native Tyre, had fallen deeply in love with him: 'his words, his face, lay fast in her heart'. Venus and Juno came to an agreement, and while Aeneas and Dido were out hunting, Juno sent heavy rain which led them to take shelter in a cave, where love was consummated. This, says the poet, was the cause of death and evil: all winter the lovers thought of nothing but themselves. Finally, Jupiter put an end to the affair. He sent Mercury (Hermes) to remind Aeneas that his destiny did not lie in Carthage and that he must stop building the walls and houses of Carthage, which was to be the enemy of the city he must build in Italy. Aeneas found himself in a quandary; he wanted to obey the god's command, but did not know how to depart from Dido. He told his companions to prepare to sail secretly, while he tried to find a way to break the news gently. But Dido was not deceived. Rumour (on which Virgil has a scintillating passage) warned her of the preparations being made; she reproached Aeneas for trying to leave by stealth, forswearing their love and leaving her at the mercy of those whose enmity she had incurred by her alliance with the Trojan exile. God-fearing Aeneas, though grief-stricken, hardened his heart and returned to his ships, with the magnificent condemnation of Dido ringing in his ears. He sailed away, and as he went, he saw the walls of Carthage lit by flames, though he did not know that Dido had killed herself and the flames arose from her funeral pyre. (Virgil's readers would, of course, have drawn the obvious and intended parallel with Antony and Cleopatra, a very recent love affair in which, through his neglect of patriotic duty, Antony as well as Cleopatra had come to a bad end.)

The narrative of Virgil's epic of the founding of Rome, *The Aeneid*, properly begins with the episode of the Wooden Horse and the sack of Troy. This Pompeian fresco shows the welcome given to the Wooden Horse by the Trojans.

After leaving Dido, Aeneas returned to Acestes' kingdom in Sicily, where he had left some of his companions before he was diverted to Carthage. As it was the anniversary of his father's death, he commemorated that event with the customary funeral games. Despite the burning of his ships by the Trojan women, who were tired of travelling and anxious to settle down in the country of the friendly Acestes, and were driven to arson by the promptings of Juno, Aeneas, having called successfully on Jupiter to put out the fires, set off again for Italy, to consult the Sibyl, as advised by the shade of Anchises who appeared to him in Sicily. With the loss of one man, Palinurus, who fell overboard and drowned – the result of a pact made on Aeneas' behalf with Neptune, that the sacrifice of one life should ensure the safety of the rest – Aeneas passed the rock of the Sirens, now silent, and came to Cumae.

The Sibyl forecast 'war, war, fearful war', in which the Tiber would run with blood, but advised persistence, which would be crowned with success. Aeneas, in obedience to the suggestion of the shade of Anchises, acked to meet his father in the Underworld, and the Sibyl volunteered to guide him, after warning him that while the road to Hell is easy, the road back is a very different proposition. In order to gain entrance, however, he had to obtain the Golden Bough, as a gift for Proserpine (Persephone). Two doves, the birds of Venus, guided him to the tree that bore the Golden Bough, and led by the Sibyl, Aeneas descended into Hell: 'through the darkness, and the land of Nothing, as though walking on a woodland path under a dim moon, when black night has driven all the colours from the earth'.

After passing a ghostly host of monsters of various kinds, which caused Aeneas to brandish his sword, as though steel would repel such insubstantial creatures, they came upon Charon, filthy and squalid, his beard matted and untrimmed, poling his coal-grey boat with its load of dead. Among the dead waiting to cross was Palinurus, drowned on the voyage to Italy. On the other side was Cerberus, whom the Sibyl drugged with 'a sleepy titbit steeped in honey'. The sound of the wailing of those who had died in infancy, and of those executed for

Aeneas sacrificing the white sow to Juno, marking his arrival at his destined place in Italy. A detail from the Altar of Peace built in Rome during the reign of Augustus.

crimes they had not committed, and of those who had taken their own lives, assaulted their ears. No more cheerful were the women who had died for love, Procris, Phaedra, Pasiphae – and Dido. Aeneas beheld his lover with tears, learning for the first time that the rumour of her death was true, and called on the gods as witnesses that he had left her against his will. Dido would not look at him, and fled into the depths of the dark wood.

They reached the field where dwelt the ghosts of former warriors, including many of the heroes of the Trojan War. Deiphobus explained how he had been chopped to pieces by Menelaus and Odysseus after Helen had taken all the weapons out of his house. The Sibyl urged Aeneas not to linger and they moved on, passing the iron walls that confined the Titans and others who were expunging their offences to the gods through perpetual torments.

Finally, they arrived in a green and pleasant land, the blessed land of Elysium, where Aeneas came face to face with his father. Anchises explained that some of the spirits in Elysium would return to earth, purged of all memory by a drink from Lethe, the river of forgetfulness. Among them would be the descendants of Aeneas himself; and Anchises began to foretell the history of Rome – 'what a folk from Italy the world awaits' – while the future characters stood before them. This long recital, beginning with the son of Aeneas, culminated in 'the man of whom you have often heard tell, Augustus Caesar, sprung from Jupiter to bring again a golden age to Latium' (thus fulfilling the poet's propagandistic purpose on behalf of his patron). Anchises also told Aeneas of more immediate events, and of the wars that he himself would see. Then, by the ivory Gate of Sleep, Aeneas and the Sibyl departed from the Underworld. Aeneas rejoined his comrades, and they set a course straight for the mouth of the Tiber.

Latinus, the king of Latium and a descendant of Saturn, had been advised by the spirit of his father that he should marry his daughter, Lavinia, to a foreigner. He therefore welcomed Aeneas; 'here was the son foretold by fate, the wanderer from a distant land', who would 'raise our blood to the stars'. But, meanwhile, Juno had observed the

Above, left:
Dido abandoned by Aeneas, whose departing ship is visible at the top. A Pompeian wall painting.

Above:
The entrance to the shrine of the Sybil at Cumae. Oracular pronouncements, often of debatable meaning, were made here, as at Delphi, and it was the Sybil who, in *The Aeneid,* showed Aeneas the way to the Underworld.

165

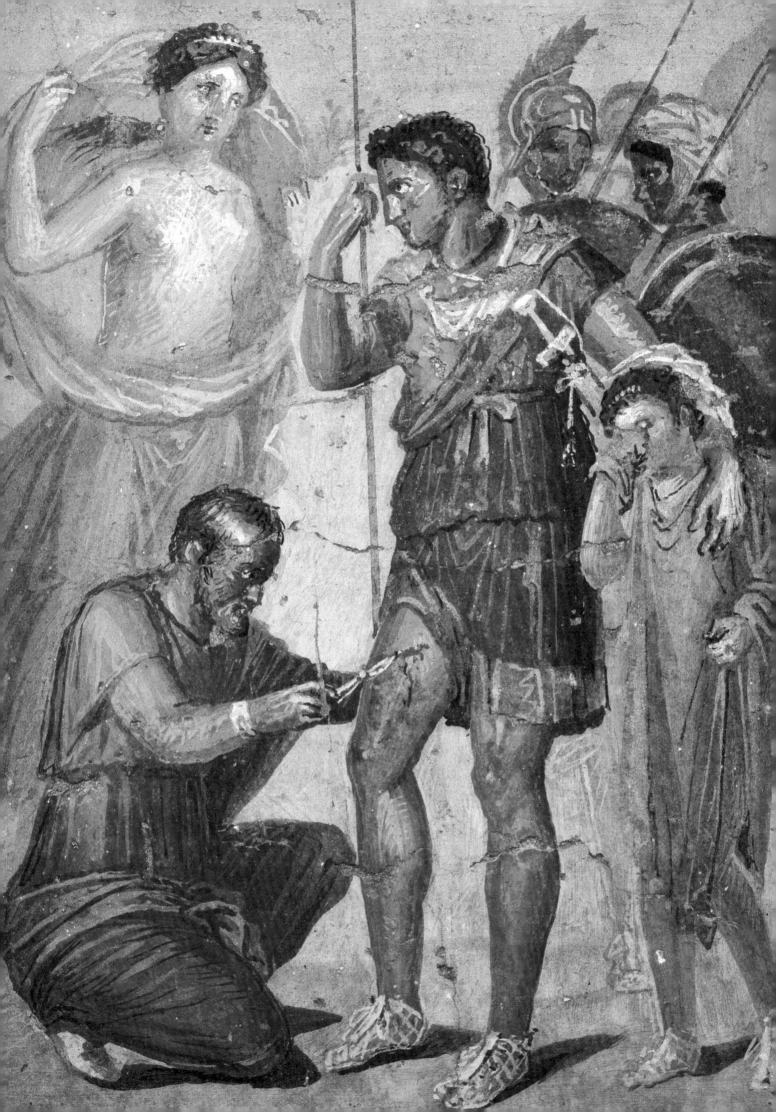

safe arrival of the Trojans in Latium in spite of all the obstacles she had thrown in their way, and bitterly wondered what use her godhead was if she were unable to stop them. Realizing she could not halt destiny, she vowed that at least the bridal price would be bloody, and the warfare that followed was largely provoked by her.

The Queen of Latium favoured another suitor, Turnus, prince of the Rutulians, whom, with the aid of Dionysiac spells, she incited to resistance; being partly of non-Latin origin, Turnus claimed to be the foreign suitor destined for Lavinia. The chance killing of a tame hart sparked off a fight against the Trojans, and King Latinus reluctantly declared war against them. Aeneas found himself confronted by a hostile alliance of the Rutulians, the Latins and others, but he managed to acquire allies himself. For as Aeneas slept, the local god, Father Tiber, appeared to him in a dream, urged him to stand fast – 'this is your dwelling place, the home of your Household Gods' – and to seek an alliance with Evander, ruler of an Arcadian colony on what was to be the Palatine Hill. Next morning, his vision confirmed by the discovery of a sow with white piglets as Father Tiber had promised, Aeneas set off up river to seek Evander, whom he found engaged in festivities devoted to Hercules (Heracles). Evander explained how Hercules had performed one of his most notable feats in that very place.

This was the destruction of a monster named Cacus. Cacus apparently abducted some of the cattle of Geryon, while Hercules was resting on the Aventine Hill on his way back with the herd which he had taken from Geryon (in his Tenth Labour). Cacus dragged them by the tail to his cave, but their lowing betrayed their hiding place to Hercules, who forced his way into the cave, killed Cacus, and retrieved the missing beasts. He left instructions that festivities should be held for him at what became Rome, and, in various different stories, left certain followers behind who are sometimes numbered among the founders of Rome. There is some evidence that Cacus was an ancient god; he is said to have had a sister whose worship was similar to that of Vesta. Alternatively, since 'smoke billowed from his mouth', he may represent dim memories of a volcanic eruption–a possible reason why Rome was settled comparatively late.

A marble fountain in the Capitoline Museum representing Tiberinus, Father Tiber, the god of the river.

Evander took Aeneas on a conducted tour of the district, an opportunity for Virgil to expand on the history, geography and mythology of Rome: the Capitol, for example, 'all golden now, but in those ancient times covered with wild scrub' and inhabited by a god whose identity Evander could not tell. Finally, Aeneas took advantage of Evander's humble hospitality, sleeping on a bed of leaves covered with a bearskin. While he slept, his mother Venus was lying with her husband, Vulcan (Hephaestus), whom she persuaded to make arms for Aeneas.

Evander agreed to help Aeneas, and Venus appeared bringing the arms that Vulcan and the Cyclops had made; the shield was engraved with future Roman triumphs, from Romulus to Augustus. But meanwhile, Juno had sent a message to Turnus to tell him that now was his chance to attack. The Rutulians stormed the Trojan stronghold and attempted to burn their ships, which were turned into sea nymphs at the instigation of the goddess Cybele, since they had been made from her sacred pine trees. Turnus was undaunted by this sign of divine support for Aeneas, and compared himself with the sons of Atreus, who had also been robbed of a wife by a Trojan prince. He swore he would require no wooden horse to defeat his enemy.

The Trojans remained on the defensive, as Aeneas had advised them, but two of them, Nissus and Euryalus, seeking glory, volunteered to slip out and warn Aeneas of Turnus' attack. On their way through the sleeping enemy, they surprised and killed many of the Rutulians. The young Euryalus was carried away with the lust for killing, but Nissus finally dragged him away. They gained the road beyond, but Latin horsemen spotted them by the moonlight glinting on Euryalus' helmet. As they made their escape, Euryalus became lost in the tangled woods. Nissus went back for him, and both were caught and killed.

When 'Aurora left Tithonus' saffron bed', the fighting was renewed. Turnus broke through the Trojan defences and killed many, including Pandarus, whose head he cleaved in two. But the Trojans were rallied by Mnestheus, and the hard-pressed Turnus eventually had to leap into the river to escape.

Meanwhile, Jupiter summoned a council on Olympus to discuss the situation in Italy. Venus spoke strongly in favour of Aeneas and

Diana the Huntress, as depicted in a Roman-period statue found at Ephesus. She was the goddess of the grove where Aeneas obtained the Golden Bough which enabled him to visit the Underworld.

the Trojans; Juno deplored their activities – 'stirring peaceful folk to fight' – no less strongly. Jupiter announced that the matter should be left to the Fates.

The hard-pressed followers of Aeneas were relieved by the return of their lord, who had been informed of current events by his former ships – now sea nymphs.

Besides Evander, Aeneas secured the alliance of the Etruscans, who had rebelled against their tyrannical king, Mezentius, killed by Aeneas.

Aeneas, his sword cutting through bronze armour, did great slaughter among the Rutulians, but Pallas, the son of Evander, was killed by Turnus, after wounding the Rutulian chief superficially with a spear. In an effort to save her favourite from his pre-ordained death, Juno took on the appearance of Aeneas and lured Turnus on board a ship to carry him away from the fighting. During a truce, a popular movement grew among the war-torn Latins to settle the contest by single combat between Aeneas and Turnus, who was restored to the war by his own wish. But Turnus insisted on a renewal of the battle, in which the Amazonian queen, Camilla, 'awful maiden', performed great deeds, though causing only distress to Diana (Artemis) who foresaw the death of her favourite. She was indeed ambushed by Arruns, on whom the vengeance of Diana soon fell, for he was killed by an arrow fired by another of Diana's companions, Opis.

Aeneas and his allies had the best of this renewed encounter and, during another truce, Turnus agreed to fight a duel with Aeneas. The efforts of Latinus and Queen Amata to negotiate a peaceful settlement Turnus ignored. Juno prompted Turnus' sister, Juturna, to incite the Rutulians to break the truce and attack Aeneas treacherously, but Venus made his wound heal swiftly. Meanwhile, Aeneas promised that, if victorious, he would treat the Latins well, leaving Latinus as king and founding a new city named for Lavinia; and Jupiter comforted Juno by ordaining that the new nations should afterwards be united.

Then the last act commenced, the duel between Aeneas and Turnus, its issue in little doubt. Turnus lost his sword and fled, but Aeneas found he could not draw his spear from a tree sacred to Faunus (Pan), where he had stuck it, and a kindly nymph provided Turnus with a new sword. But Turnus was doomed and Juturna, seeing the gods were against her brother, drowned herself. Aeneas wounded Turnus in the leg and brought him to the ground. The stricken Rutulian prince begged that his body might be sent back to his father, and Aeneas, whose heart was softening, might have spared his rival had he not suddenly noticed that he was wearing, as spoils of war, the belt of Pallas. Angered then, he thrust home, and the spirit of Turnus, with a groan, fled from his body.

Virgil's poem, which he is traditionally said to have wanted destroyed when he died, ends with the death of Turnus. Aeneas subsequently married Lavinia and founded Lavinium; the Latins retained their own identity, while accepting the gods of Aeneas. The towns of Laurentum (Latinus' city) and Lavinium remained important religious centres in later times.

The *Aeneid* is not, of course, genuine mythology, because much of it is the conscious creation of the poet; some of the characters appear to have been invented totally by Virgil and some scenes are obvious political propaganda—such as Anchises' recital of the glorious future of Rome in Book VI which resembles in purpose the archbishop's speech over the infant Elizabeth in Shakespeare's *Henry VIII*. However, the national epic enshrined in the *Aeneid* existed long before Virgil, who drew extensively on the works of earlier writers; most of Roman literature is to a great extent an expression of patriotism. Aeneas himself, who in Virgil is a personification of the stoic ideal of the honourable man fulfilling his destiny by overcoming the difficulties life places in his way, had figured as a founder of Italian cities as early as the 6th century B.C., and was possibly associated with Rome in the 5th century, though the legend cannot be found in recognizable form until the 3rd century. A King Latinus is mentioned by Hesiod, though Virgil was responsible for encumbering him with numerous divine forefathers, including Saturn. There were numerous other versions of the story told in the *Aeneid* in which the chief characters are the same but their relationships are different: Latinus is sometimes the friend of Aeneas, for example, sometimes the opponent.

The tradition that Aeneas was the forefather of the Romans posed a certain chronological difficulty when the legend of Romulus, the actual founder of the city, was taken into account. The Romans of historical times knew that their city was founded in the mid 8th century B.C. or thereabouts (an earlier estimate was 814 B.C.). Although they could not date the Trojan War precisely, they knew that Troy fell somewhere about 1190, and therefore the arrival of Aeneas in Latium must have occurred well over 300 years before Romulus. This slightly embarrassing gap was overcome by the characteristically ingenious

The god Mars visits Rhea Silvia while she is asleep. Detail from a Roman marble relief in the Lateran Museum.

An Etruscan painted terracotta head of Hermes. The Romans took one of his aspects – patron of traders and merchants – and made him into their god Mercury. However, Mercury performs one of Hermes' duties – as a messenger of the gods – in *The Aeneid*.

structure of Roman historians, and it did at least offer opportunities for the invention of a whole series of mythical rulers from whom patrician families could claim to be descended. None of these characters is much more than a name.

According to the Roman historians, notably Livy, the Latin people evolved from the fusion of the original, relatively uncivilized Latins, with Aeneas' Trojans. After the death of Aeneas in Lavinium, his son started a new settlement at Alba Longa. Two of his descendants, Numitor and Amulius, twin brothers, quarrelled over who should rule, and Numitor was driven out. His male relations were killed and his only female relation, Rhea Silvia, was forced to become a Vestal Virgin, taking an oath of eternal chastity. Thus Amulius made his line safe, as he thought; but Rhea Silvia was raped by Mars (Livy is far from certain that Mars was guilty), and Amulius had her thrown into prison. She gave birth to twin sons, Romulus and Remus, who were exposed, perhaps like Moses in a basket on the river. (Twins have a powerful mystique and occur in the myths of many peoples; it appears that Remus did not belong in the earliest version of the legend, or at least that he was not the twin brother of Romulus).

Romulus and Remus suckled
by the she-wolf, on the bank of
the Tiber (represented by the
figure at bottom right). An eagle
watches, as they are discovered
by shepherds.

A she-wolf, on her way to drink at the Tiber, came upon the
stranded basket; she suckled the babies and licked them clean.
(Sceptics in Rome were fond of pointing out that *lupa*, the word for
a she-wolf, could also mean a prostitute). Plutarch (about A.D. 100)
says the protecting creature was a woodpecker, the bird of Mars. A
herdsman, Faustulus, perhaps to be identified with Faunus, the
Roman Pan, found the children under the wolf's protection and took
them home to his wife, whose name, Larentia, suggests a connection
with the Lares, the Roman household gods. The boys grew up and
became Robin Hoods of a kind, attacking robbers and dividing their
plunder with the shepherds among whom they lived. At some point,
Remus was captured and delivered to Amulius, who handed him
over to Numitor, now ruling an adjacent and inferior kingdom. He
was, of course, the grandfather (or uncle) of the twins, and the truth
about their birth was revealed. Thereupon they killed Amulius and,
having restored Numitor to his throne, set off to found a city of their
own, since Alba Longa had become over-populated.

However, the same problem arose that had afflicted their predecessors, for the two brothers quarrelled over who was to rule the new
city. They decided to seek a decision by augury of the local gods (the
Roman passion for auguries derived from the Etruscans), and took up
their positions on the Palatine and Aventine hills. Six birds descended

to the Aventine Hill, where Remus stood, but twelve then alighted by Romulus on the Palatine. This failed to solve the problem, for Remus claimed priority while Romulus claimed superiority. Angry words followed, and Remus was killed by his brother. The Romans were troubled by this act of fratricide on the part of their illustrious founder, and in his version of the story Ovid absolved Romulus from blame by making one of his followers the murderer of Remus, striking him down with a spade when he mockingly jumped over the half-built walls which Romulus had thrown up by ploughing a furrow around the Palatine.

Rome grew up initially on the Palatine Hill, where in Livy's own time (Livy was a contemporary of Virgil) a little round mud-walled hut said to have been the hut of Romulus was still preserved. Archaeological evidence suggests that the structure of this hut was an authentic 8th-century reproduction; an Iron Age hut has been found under the Palatine Hill. Romulus gave the city strong fortifications, good laws and a body of 100 senators, the ancestors of the patricians of Rome. He also established a sanctuary for fugitives on the Capitoline Hill.

Like other pioneer settlements, Rome was handicapped by a predominance of men, and it was to rectify the situation that the people of Romulus carried out their famous raid on a neighbouring tribe, the Sabines. Attempts to arrange peaceful marriages had failed owing to the suspicions of the new city that Rome's neighbours harboured, and a plan was laid to obtain women by force. Grand festivities were organized in celebration of Neptune, which attracted many visitors, particularly the Sabines, but as the games were at their height a signal was given and the Romans began seizing all the young women. Particularly good-looking girls had been marked down for the senators; otherwise, it was a free-for-all. Protests were in vain, and the Sabines had to depart without their daughters.

The girls were, of course, thoroughly alarmed, but Romulus assured them that they would be treated respectfully, as Roman wives, not concubines, while the Roman captors assured their prisoners that the kidnapping had been inspired by uncontrollable desire. The result was that the Sabine girls soon became reconciled to their fate. Not so their fathers, however, and the first Roman war was fought over the Rape of the Sabine Women.

The Latins were soon forced on to the defensive, and the Sabines gained entry to the city through the alleged treachery of a Latin girl, Tarpeia. No sooner had she let the Sabine warriors into the city than they crushed her to death with their shields – to show that no obligations were due to a traitor, or alternatively to make the Romans think they had gained an entrance to the city by force alone. (Another version relates how Tarpeia had asked in payment for her help what the Sabines wore on their shield arms; she was referring to their gold bracelets, but they chose to interpret her demand differently.) The Tarpeian Rock, from which traitors to Rome were hurled to their

Romulus and Remus. A marble medallion on the Certosa di Pavia façade.

The Rape of the Sabine Women – an ever-popular subject with artists. Frieze from the Basilica Aemiliana in the Forum.

The temple of Romulus on the Via Sacra in the Forum. The building dates from the fourth century A.D. and the original doors are intact with locks in working order. It is doubtful now whether the dedicatee was in fact the legendary founder of Rome: evidence suggests that the Romulus named was the son of the emperor Maxentius.

deaths, was named after Rome's first traitor. The Sabines having captured the citadel (despite intervention by Janus, who let loose a cascade of hot water), the decisive battle was about to begin, when the Sabine women, showing every sign of distress, threw themselves between the contending armies and besought peace between their husbands and their fathers. Their plea was effective, peace was made, and thenceforth the Sabines and the Latins became one people, with Rome their capital and Sabines among Rome's early kings. Romulus built a temple in the Forum to Jupiter Stator, 'Stayer of Flight', because in answer to his prayer Jupiter had made the Romans stand fast when the Sabines attacked.

It was during the Sabine Wars that Lake Curtius, the swampy area in the Forum, gained its name. Curtius was originally a Sabine soldier who rode his horse into the lake and was drowned. Alternatively, Curtius narrowly avoided drowning, after his horse stumbled into the lake. Or—a third possibility—a chasm opened in the place where the lake was subsequently formed and a young Roman named Curtius leapt into it as a sacrifice to the gods of the city; the chasm then closed up again.

Romulus took part in various other minor wars as king of Rome, until one day he vanished in a thunderstorm before the eyes of all the people, who promptly acclaimed him a god. (This apotheosis is somewhat at odds with the existence of the alleged burial place of Romulus—a grim little corner of the Forum.) He was worshipped under the name of Quirinus, probably an old Sabine god, in historical Rome, and his chief place of worship was the Quirinal Hill, an early Sabine settlement. His godly functions overlapped with those of Mars, for Quirinus too was a War-god, whose arms were anointed by the priests in an obscure ritual.

A Sabine king was briefly associated with Romulus in joint rule, but he seems to have disappeared again quite rapidly. Traditionally, six kings followed Romulus in the period between his death and the foundation of the Republic in 510 B.C., the earlier ones Sabines and the later ones Etruscans. It is very difficult to disentangle history from myth in this period. It seems likely that early Rome was ruled by kings and certain that there was a period of Etruscan dominance, but whether the kings were real individuals is more doubtful. The balancing of a 'good' Tarquin against a 'bad' Tarquin seems a shade too neat for historical reality, and other aspects of the kings are clearly the result of myth-making on the part of Roman writers.

The first Sabine king, Numa Pompilius, was a counterpart to the warlike Romulus, being a man of peace and the organizer of religion in Rome. He was said to have been a pupil of Pythagoras, though that was chronologically impossible. At any rate, just as Romulus represents Roman practical efficiency and physical action, Numa represents the broad, receptive interest in the supernatural which in the course of time embraced so many different beliefs. Numa was believed to have built the temple of Janus in the Forum, to have introduced the worship of Minerva, and to have instituted orders of priests, including the *flamines* who attended the major deities, and the post of Pontifex Maximus, a high priest who supervised the correct forms of worship, particularly that of Vesta. To Numa's influence was ascribed the important Roman quality of piety – the English word fails to convey its full meaning, which included the assiduous practice of religious and social customs. Numa had the benefit of a private line to the gods through a nymph called Aegereia, possibly his wife, whom he consulted on dark nights in her grotto.

An amusing story was told of how Numa, by his quick wits, made Jupiter settle for a less exorbitant ritual sacrifice than the god was about to demand. Aegereia told him how to capture the two rustic gods, Faunus and Picus, which he did by leaving wine near a fountain. (This seems to have been adopted from the method of Midas to capture Silenus.) They showed him how to summon Jupiter, and Numa asked the god what he required by way of sacrifice when he sent his admonitory thunderbolts. Jupiter began by saying 'A head . . .' at which Numa hastily put in 'of garlic'. The god went on 'Human . . .', and Numa added 'hair'. Again Jupiter began, 'The life of . . .', 'a sprat' Numa exclaimed. So amused was Jupiter by Numa's cleverness, that he allowed these very things – a head of garlic, human hair, and a small fish – to be sufficient sacrifices.

Numa's two successors, Tullus Hostilius and Ancus Marcius, had similar functions as founders of religious customs, law and justice. It has been suggested that, while Tullus may well have been an historical character, Ancus was more likely an invention designed to provide the powerful family of the Marcii with an impressive ancestor.

The legend of the Horatii and the Curiatii was ascribed to the reign of Tullus Hostilius. Rome was at war with Alba Longa, and both sides agreed that the conflict should be decided by a fight between three champions from each side. Two sets of brothers were chosen, the Horatii for Rome and the Curiatii for Alba Longa; all six had been born on the same day. As the two armies looked on, two of the Horatii were killed and the third forced to flee. However, all three of the Curatii had been wounded in different ways, and as they pursued the fleeing Roman their various physical incapacities caused them to become widely separated. When he judged the space between his pursuers was large enough, Horatius suddenly turned and, fighting each of the Curiatii individually, killed them all.

It happened that a sister of Horatius was betrothed to one of the Curatii, and when she saw her brother returning with her lover's cloak, which she had made, flung over his shoulder, she realized what had happened and broke into cries of woe, calling upon the gods to take her life also. In rage that his triumph should provoke such a reaction, Horatius ran his sword through her. For this murder he was condemned to death, but an eloquent plea for mercy by his father resulted in his release by a popular assembly. The legend appears to account for the origin of the right of an accused Roman to appeal to the people.

Tullus Hostilius's reign came to an end when Jupiter destroyed him and his entire household with a thunderbolt. The king had been meddling in sacred rites for which he was not qualified, in an attempt to discover the source of a plague.

The reign of Lucius Tarquinius Priscus, traditionally dated 616–578 B.C., introduces the period of Etruscan dominance. (Though Rome probably had an Etruscan dynasty and was certainly much influenced by Etruscan customs, it probably did not belong to the league of Etruscan cities.) At that time Rome first became a large and powerful city, the equal of the Etruscan cities in the north. The first Tarquin is said by Livy to have been a Greek refugee who settled in Etruria and gained the Roman crown when he superseded the sons of Ancus Marcius, who had been his pupils. He was credited with great building works, including the famous sewers and the temple of Jupiter on the Capitoline, completed later.

Tarquin was said to have been responsible for the acquisition of the Sibylline Books, the recorded oracular pronouncements of the prophetess at Cumae, who corresponded to the Delphic oracle in Greece. Cumae was an early Greek colony in Italy, famous for the worship of Apollo, the only major deity who is identical in both Greek and Roman mythology. Various explanations were given of the origin of the first Sibyl at Cumae. It was said, for example, that she was a Trojan woman (this fitted in well with the story of Aeneas), who had resided at Erythrae, in Asia Minor, before she came to Cumae. Apollo granted her long life on condition that she never touched the soil of Erythrae again, and she lived to be very old before she received a message from her old home containing a trace of Erythraean soil. When she touched it, the Sibyl died at once. Others say that Apollo's gift was immortality without the necessary addition of perpetual youth, and that the Sibyl ended as a little dried-up creature like a grasshopper, who lived in a cage and answered inquiries about her wishes with the statement that she wished only to die.

The Sibyl had a considerable influence on Roman affairs, from her conduct of Aeneas to the Underworld until comparatively late historical times. She was responsible for the import of the worship of several Greek deities, including Demeter (as Ceres), Hermes (Mercury) and Poseidon (Neptune), at various times in order to deal with some catastrophe, such as a famine, with which the Roman gods seemed unable or unwilling to cope. During the Second Punic War (218–201 B.C.), for example, it was as a result of consulting the Sibylline Books that the cult of Cybele was brought to Rome.

Tarquin was succeeded by Servius Tullius, apparently a native Roman from the plebeian colony on the Aventine Hill, whose qualities were revealed by fire flickering around his head. The myths associated with him resemble those told of Romulus. He built the city wall, reorganized Roman society on a property basis, drew the cities of Latium into a Roman league, and built the temple of Diana on the Aventine (it has been suggested that Servius was actually a priest of

Diana). He established a festival in honour of the Lares, and one legend said he was the son of the household god (Lar) of the first Tarquin. Another tradition, embraced by the learned Emperor Claudius, held that Servius was an Etruscan. A popular legend gave him a miraculous birth: a phallic shape appeared in the royal hearth and a female slave, Ocrisia, who was a foreign princess captured in war, became pregnant as she sat by the fire and in due time gave birth to the future king.

Tullius came to a nasty end, according to another legend. His daughter, Tullia, had married one of the superseded Tarquin princes, and took her husband's side in a plot against her father. Tullius was assassinated, and his evil daughter drove her chariot over his body as it lay in the road.

At any rate, he was followed by the second Tarquin, Tarquinius Superbus, 'the Proud', whom some see as merely the alter ego of Tarquinius Priscus. On succeeding to the crown of his—possible—father-in-law, Tarquin swiftly reversed the democratically inclined reforms of Servius, decimated the senate and instituted a repressive tyranny. Most of the well-known myths concerning the Tarquins are probably Greek in influence if not in origin, and though some may be closely related to facts, others are clearly not. For example, the evidence suggests that Rome acquired dominion over the town of Gabii by peaceful means, not by the colourful exploits of violence and treachery ascribed to Tarquin and his son, Sextus.

Sextus went to Gabii, against which Tarquin had waged an unsuccessful war, with a story that he was fleeing from his father's despotism, and sought political asylum. He was well-received, and became friendly with the leaders of Gabii, so that he learned everything about the town. When he felt that he was securely ensconced, he sent a messenger in secret to his father in Rome to ask what he should do next. The messenger repeated the question to Tarquin who, perhaps suspicious that he might be a spy, gave no answer, and strolled out into the garden. The messenger followed him there and asked again what were his instructions for Sextus. Still Tarquin remained silent, walking up and down and knocking the heads of the poppies off their stems with a staff he carried. The exasperated messenger finally gave up, and returned to Gabii where he recounted Tarquin's odd behaviour to Sextus. But Sextus at once interpreted his father's meaning, and proceeded to organize the assassination of the leaders of Gabii, which then passed under Rome's control.

There was more than one legendary explanation for the name of Lake Curtius in Rome. According to the most popular version, it derived its name from Marcus Curtius, who rode into the yawning chasm as a sacrifice for the people of Rome. Roman marble relief.

Above, left:
Tarpeia meets the fate courted by all traitors—destruction at the hands of the enemy they serve, in this case the Sabine soldiers.

177

Numa Pompilius, the legendary king of Rome who negotiated so effectively with Jupiter on behalf of the people. A statue of the 2nd century A.D. from the House of the Vestals.

Tarquin had two other sons, Titus and Arruns, whom he sent to consult Apollo's oracle at Delphi concerning the meaning of an omen – a snake had emerged from a column in the temple of Jupiter on the Capitoline Hill. They were accompanied by Lucius Junius Brutus, a nephew of Tarquin who had survived the jealous slaughter of the rest of his family by pretending to be stupid; hence, possibly, his surname. At Delphi, the young men took the opportunity of asking another question which interested them more deeply than the matter of the snake and the column: who would be the next king of Rome? The oracle answered: he who shall first kiss his mother. Titus and Arruns drew lots to decide which one of them should perform this honour, having agreed not to tell Sextus, the third brother, anything about it. But while they were thus making their plans, Brutus, in his bumbling way, fell over and while prostrate bestowed a kiss on Mother Earth.

On their return, the brothers found their comrades encamped near the town of Ardea, which was under siege. During the military stalemate the well-born young men spent the evenings in luxurious entertainment and in talking about women. All of them loyally praised the virtue and responsibility of their own wives, but one member of the party, Collatinus, suggested that they should pay a surprise visit to Rome to see if their wives' behaviour was as virtuous as their absent husbands alleged. When they got there, they found the ladies having a party of their own, in the company of handsome young men. The only exception was the beautiful wife of Collatinus himself, Lucretia, who was discovered, alone with her maidservants, sewing (the one form of labour that Roman wives were expected to undertake).

The youngest of the Tarquins, Sextus, was so impressed by Lucretia that he determined to enjoy her. Some days later he came secretly to the house and, when Lucretia resisted his advances, swore that he would kill her and one of the male servants, to create the impression that they had been lovers. Lucretia then had no choice but to submit. When Sextus had gone, she summoned her father and her husband, told them what had happened, and then killed herself with a knife thrust. One of the witnesses to her recital of her wrongs was Brutus, who took the lead in the outcry that was raised against the Tarquins, and swore that there should be no more kings in Rome. By the time that Tarquin returned from Ardea to nip the insurrection in the bud, the gates of Rome were barred against him. He and his sons went into exile, Sextus choosing rather oddly to go to Gabii, where he was assassinated. In Rome, the monarchy was replaced by the consular system – two consuls elected by popular vote. The first men to hold the office were Brutus and Collatinus.

Rome had not seen the end of the Tarquinian menace. Collatinus was to resign his consulship and go into exile because he was a kinsman of the Tarquins. At about the same time Brutus ordered the execution of his own sons for plotting to restore the monarchy. Tarquin himself had sought an alliance with an Etruscan king, Lars Porsena, whose army marched against a weakened Rome. The Romans retreated before the Etruscan advance, fleeing across the bridge that crossed the Tiber, which the Etruscans had to capture intact in order to capture the city. The guard at the bridge, Horatius Cocles ('One-Eyed'), called to the fleeing Romans to stand with him, but only two men answered his call. Together the three held the bridge against the first attack of the Etruscans. Others were hurriedly demolishing the structure, and as it neared collapse they called to Horatius to save himself. He sent his two companions to safety and stood alone on the bridge against the Etruscans. Then, as the bridge finally fell, Horatius dived into the river, where Father Tiber preserved him from harm.

Roman Religion. State and Household

The vast power and prestige of Rome in the 2nd century B.C., and the speed with which it had risen to its contemporary status, seemed nothing less than miraculous – to Romans and to intelligent foreign observers equally. Some might say merely that Rome enjoyed the favour of the gods, and leave it at that, but others discerned the reasons for Rome's eminence in the moral qualities of Roman civilization. How closely the two factors were connected was a moot point.

The trinity of Roman virtues, *virtus*, *pietas*, *fides*, signified self-discipline and strength of character, respect for the order of things, and honour, good faith, the keeping of agreements. At that time (i.e. the 2nd century B.C.) Rome was coming under the fertile influence of Greek philosophy, yet the basic moral qualities of the Romans were to change very little. Stoicism, indeed, closely approached Roman ideals, while adding a much-needed humanizing influence.

As in other nations, the universally upheld public virtues were no doubt less evident in day-to-day behaviour, but they were formidable nonetheless. It was a natural development for the Romans to project them backwards in time, to suppose the earliest development of the city resulted from adherence to these ideals; in a word, to make a myth out of them.

Perhaps the dominant imperative in the Roman notion of virtue was devotion to the state, an idea far more complex than what we would call patriotism, involving the acceptance and support of the whole social order. The first duty of the citizen was to the group of which he was a member. The individual was always subservient, his interests inferior. This was true of all social groups within the state, but the most important institutions were the state itself and its microcosm, the family. Thus the consul Brutus, ordering the death of his own sons when they were found guilty of acting against the state, was grandly fulfilling his obligations. Thus, too, the warrior Curtius, leaping into the chasm, offered himself as a sacrifice for the good of the state; and the legendary consul, Genucius Cipus, went into voluntary exile to save the Republic when it was prophesied that he would be the next king of Rome.

The Romans put great value in the order and permanence of things (and, to mention the most obvious example, built their roads accordingly). The existing order had to be maintained, everything had to happen at the right time and in the right place: stability and security were the aims. Innovations were regarded with suspicion.

The Romans were not a very imaginative people, and their values were concrete values, not abstract concepts. Honour was attained by action, not by vague aspiration; piety was achieved by correct performance of one's obligations. Roman morality had practically

The emperor Augustus wearing the veil of the Pontifex Maximus, or chief priest. The office was held by Julius Caesar and by the emperors thereafter.

This charming pair of buildings near the Ponte Rotto in Rome are traditionally called the temple of Vesta (the round one) and the temple of Fortuna Virilis. The Romans were painstaking about rendering due respect to a large number of gods and spirits, and temples proliferated as the city grew. Some are now unidentified, and neither of these temples can be named with certainty.

nothing to do with religion; indeed, Roman religion can be regarded merely as 'an emanation of the principles of social order and moral restraint that guided the people in their everyday lives' (Peter Arnott).

There is an apparent paradox between the comparatively non-religious nature of the Romans on the one hand, and the profusion of their religious rites, festivals and cults on the other. (Ovid attempted a calendar of all Roman religious festivals, but only managed to complete six months of the year, which filled six books.)

The complex Roman calendar was ascribed to King Numa. Before him it included only ten months, January and February being ignored. The names of the months had religious associations; the first month of the year was the month of Mars, March. April was the month of 'opening' when the flowers opened, May was named after the ancient goddess who later became more or less subsumed in her successor in the calendar, Juno. The rest of the months were numbered – October is the eighth month, November the ninth. July and August gained their names in imperial times, when the calendar was reformed, and commemorated the Caesars, Julius and Augustus. When January and February were introduced, during or soon after the time of Numa, they were clearly meant to come first, as January was dedicated to the two-faced Janus, god of beginnings, but in fact March continued to be the first month of the Roman year until the middle of the 2nd century B.C. February was named for the ceremony of *februalia*, the propitiation of the dead.

The months were based on the moon and were divided up by 'kalends', the beginning, 'nones', the middle, and 'ides', full moon. Days were numbered by reference to those points in the month.

Their possession of a calendar meant that the Roman religious festivals were organized on a regular, planned basis, and reinforced the identity of religion and the state. Festivals were remarkably numerous (more so, even, than religious festivals in modern Italy), and tended to congregate particularly in spring and autumn – seed-time and harvest, or the start and close of the campaigning season; this was signified in March by the antics of the priests of Mars dancing with spears and twelve shields (*anciles*) which were copies of a Jovian prototype dropped from heaven in the time of Numa.

Many of the customs of early Roman religion have parallels in other cultures; they are not far removed from the beliefs and cere-monies of – for example – simple New Guinea tribesmen, and except to scholars they are of limited interest today. Roman religious customs also included a number of curious rites the precise meaning of which was as much a mystery to the Romans as it is to us. There was, for example, a curious and unpleasant ceremony that took place on the ides (15th) of October. A chariot race was run in the Campus Martius, and one of the winning horses was sacrificed to Mars. Various parts of the unfortunate animal figured in subsidiary rites. The severed head was the prize for the winners of two fighting groups, each drawn from a particular district of the city. The blood was used by the Vestal Virgins in purification rites. The tail was hung to drip blood on an altar. Probably, like most ancient and obscure customs, the origin of this ceremony was some kind of rustic fertility rite: horses were sometimes associated with corn. The grisly character of the whole business makes it tempting to assume Etruscan influence.

A purification ceremony, equally enigmatic in purpose but more attractive in character, took place on the Ides of May at the Pons Sublicius, the old wooden bridge which had once been the only crossing of the Tiber, defended by Horatius. A solemn procession (most old observances involved a procession of some kind, as religion was originally entirely an open-air affair) proceeded to the bridge where a number of straw puppets were cast into the river. One likely explanation is that this was an offering to Father Tiber by way of apology for throwing a bridge across him. The puppets may well have been substitutes for earlier human sacrifice. This was one of the few state ceremonies to which the common folk were admitted, though they took no active part.

Of special importance to the Romans was Vesta, the goddess of the hearth. The hearth was the centre of the household and the family, and the originals of the Vestal Virgins were the daughters of the king, who were responsible for tending the royal hearth. Every Roman household had its attendant spirits, of whom the most important were the Lares and Penates. The origins of the Lares, like so many other gods, were rustic. They were the guardians of farm boundaries and of crossroads, and protectors of travellers. They were represented as young men bearing fruits, and received monthly offerings of wine, bread and honey. In time they moved into the city and into individual houses. One of these household gods appears in a play by Plautus, amiably remarking to the audience that, in case anyone is wondering who he is, he will explain himself. He is, he says, the god of the house the audience have just seen him leaving. He keeps a keen and paternal watch on the whole family, and had done so for the present master's father. The daughter of the house comes to his shrine every day 'to pay her respects'; she brings a whiff of incense, wine, or some other gift, and decks him with flowers. (A daughter leaving the house to get married would offer her girlish toys to the Lar.)

The Lares were concerned with the whole affairs of the household in the widest sense, while the duties of the Penates were more narrowly defined. Brought to Rome by Aeneas, according to popular tradition, they were the guardians of the store-cupboard (*penus*).

Possibly, the original household gods were the spirits of the ancestors of the house's inhabitants. The Romans had no very vigorous belief in a life after death, but honouring one's ancestors was an important aspect of *pietas*. The spirits of the dead (*manes*) had to be propitiated by a curious rite in which the master would walk round the house spitting out beans at intervals and politely requesting the spirits to remove themselves. In funeral processions, family ancestors were sometimes represented by actors wearing masks.

According to a dubious tale related by Ovid, the Lares were the children of Mercury and Lara (or Lala), an ancient goddess connected with the Underworld. Ovid relates how Mercury took advantage of her while conveying her to the Underworld: she could not cry for help because she had been struck dumb by Jupiter, who was angry

The triumphal arch of the emperor Titus, in the Forum. The emperor was often much more than Pontifex Maximus, he was a god as well, as the inscription here makes plain.

with her for revealing the plans for one of his numerous seductions.

Another ancient goddess, of Italian origin though her myth is Greek-influenced, was Bona Dea, from whose cult men were barred. She was said to have been the daughter of Faunus, who conceived an incestuous desire for her and, when she would not yield to him, beat her to death with myrtle rods. Another version has it that she was the wife of Faunus, who administered the beating when she got drunk. Not surprisingly, myrtle was tabu in the Bona Dea cult, and so was wine: although it was used in offerings, it was described as milk.

There was a story that Hercules had come upon the worshippers of Bona Dea during his journey through Italy and had asked them for a drink, which they refused because he was a man. It was for this reason that Hercules refused to allow women to take part in his cult in Rome.

According to late writers such as Plutarch, Hercules was also involved with the cult of another old Italian goddess, Acca Larentia (who appears in another guise as stepmother of Romulus and Remus). She was a beautiful whore won by an attendant of Hercules' temple as a consolation prize, after he had lost a game of dice with the god. When she left the temple next morning, Acca Larentia was advised by Hercules to approach the first man she met in the street. He turned out to be extremely rich, and when he died he left her all his property.

Although religious worship was so prominent a feature of life in Rome, it was largely a passive affair, a matter of propitiating the gods to ensure that they did their jobs—making the corn grow, the grapes ripen, the rain fall, and so on—and as this encompassed virtually every aspect of life, the sheer number of rituals to be performed was very large. As most of them were rather pleasant, involving games, feasts and entertainments, they imposed no great social burden; as a rule, they were not very demanding in terms of sacrifices. (Neptune received small fishes, cast on to a fire.) The Romans' relationship with their gods was in this sense characteristically businesslike, a matter simply of 'contractual magic'. Cato's instructions for the propitiatory rituals to be carried out on farms were delivered in the tone of an agricultural bulletin.

It was important that these rituals should be performed without deviation from a precise form. The Iguvium Tablets, which record religious practices as early as the 4th century B.C., insist that in the rite of lustration—a purifying and protective ritual similar to the old English custom of 'beating the bounds'—the conduct of the liturgy must be perfect. The form of words had to be followed exactly, and not interrupted by exterior events. If that happened, the whole ceremony was abandoned and begun again. As an extra precaution, it was the custom in Iguvium to sacrifice one more ox than the rite required, with a prayer to Jupiter that if the ceremony had been imperfect in any way, this ox was offered in propitiation for the unnoticed fault.

Such ceremonies were normally accompanied by a more or less musical din, to blot out any unwanted or ill-ominous sounds, such as the cry of a bird. Similarly, when the priest (*flamen*) of Jupiter went abroad, he was preceded by attendants to make sure that he saw or heard nothing untoward, which might infringe the positively suffocating tabus that surrounded his person; these included regulations on changing his underwear and having his hair cut.

A religion which was not responsible for inculcating virtue and morality did not offer much spiritual inspiration (and helped to open the door for the admittance of alien religions), but if Roman religion seems spiritually somewhat stunted, it was nevertheless complex and persuasive. The Romans were sensitive to the supernatural in their environment; they were constantly aware of strange, inexplicable forces, sometimes benign, more often maleficent. Spirits, *numina*, rather than gods, were to be found everywhere, and rites of propitiation were performed for all of them. Every little feauture of the scenery – a stone lying in a field, an old tree stump, a hole in the ground – tended to have superstitious associations of some kind, and people's most ordinary activities possessed religious overtones. Hence the preoccupation with omens and the art of divination.

The Roman concern with auguries was derived from the Etruscans, who were particularly expert at divination from the entrails of animals, especially birds. Birds were in general a much-pondered source of omens, and their behaviour was carefully observed at important moments. It was significant that birds had been responsible for showing that Romulus was to be the founder of Rome. It was Romulus also, according to tradition, who founded the College of Augurs.

The purpose of divination was to discover, by expert examination of omens, the attitude of the gods towards a particular enterprise. Augurs did not prophesy results, they merely reported whether the omens were favourable or unfavourable at a given time. Unfavourable omens might lead a Roman to postpone a journey he was about to make; not to cancel it, only to wait until the omens were auspicious. However, as far as state policy was concerned, there were cynical ways of evading the inconvenience of unfavourable auspices. For example, if the priests did not notice a bad omen, and did not report it, then for practical purposes it did not exist. The general Marcellus used to travel in a covered litter to avoid seeing any evil omens that might present themselves. Another general, when the chickens that accompanied the army refused to eat (a bad omen naturally), had them thrown into the sea, exclaiming that if they would not eat they could damn well drink. Critics like Cicero condemned the crude superstition of these practices; nevertheless, divination remained an important part of the state religion right down to imperial times.

In time, the agricultural magic which was the first basis for Roman religion became less and less evident, and the native gods, chiefly Jupiter, Mars, Janus and Vesta, were joined by others – Etruscan, Greek and oriental. Minerva, as has already been mentioned, came either from the Etruscans or a native Italian people. The cults of Hercules and of the 'Heavenly Twins', Castor and Pollux, came to Rome from the neighbouring, Greek-influenced cities. The twins were said to have first appeared in Rome in 499 B.C. to announce a Roman victory over the Tarquins, in which they had fought on the side of the Romans. Their winged horses drank at a pool in the Forum, where a temple was subsequently built in their honour (the well-known relic still to be seen is of course a much later building). For some reason, Castor was more prominent in Rome than his brother; possibly this was a reflection of the superiority of Romulus to Remus.

The first shrines were simple altars, set up in the fields; the construction of temples was an Etruscan innovation. It greatly assisted the gradual personalization of the gods because, once the god had a home, he was more easily visualized as a person: the first figures of gods in human form were made for the first temples, at about the beginning of the Republic. Such gods were less frightening than the disembodied spirits they replaced.

The emergence of twelve chief deities on the Olympian pattern was also derived from the Etruscans, although the Roman twelve came to be individually identified with the Greek gods, not the dim deities of Etruria. Having adopted the Greek gods, the Romans naturally adopted their whole mythology also. The stories told of Zeus, Hera, Aphrodite, etc., became those of Jupiter, Juno and Venus.

A fresco from the house of the empress Livia, wife of Augustus, showing the sacrifice of a kid. This is a domestic ritual, with the matron of the house presiding.

Opposite :
Four antique bronzes, now in the Louvre, representing Lares Familiares, the guardian spirits of the home. The word Lar is apparently Etruscan, and meant a chief. The ancient Italian Lares were agricultural spirits, brought into the home with the growth of urban life.

Strange Gods

An altar to the Great Mother – Cybele – in the Capitoline Museum in Rome. The scene illustrates an incident during the arrival of the sacred black stone in 204 B.C. When the ship transporting it grounded hard in the mud of the Tiber, a Vestal Virgin fastened her sash to the ship and drew it easily to the Palatine Hill.

In the introduction of Greek gods to Rome, a large part was played by the Sibyl of Cumae, the oracle of Apollo. It was the Sibyl who, during a famine in 493 B.C., advised the building of a temple to Ceres, Liber and Libera, Roman versions of Demeter, Iacchos and Persephone. (Iacchos was associated with Demeter and her daughter in the cult of Eleusis; he hardly appears in mythology, however, though he is sometimes identified with Dionysus.) Later the Sibyl was responsible for the introduction of other Greek gods, including Poseidon (identified with Neptune), Hermes (Mercury) and Asklepios, whom the Romans called Aesculapius.

But the most remarkable, and the last, foreign deity introduced on the advice of the Sibyl was not Greek at all, but oriental: Cybele, the 'Great Mother' of Asia Minor. This happened in 205 B.C., during the Second Punic War, when the victories of Hannibal had seriously dented assumptions of Roman superiority and thus put a heavy strain on the traditional state religion. The introduction of so alien a goddess is historically startling and has never been satisfactorily explained. However, when the Sibylline Books were consulted, after a freak hailstorm had hit the city, in order to find some more powerful spirit to restore Rome's invincibility, the answer was that Hannibal would be compelled to leave Italy if Cybele were brought to Rome. Accordingly, an impressive delegation was sent to Pessinus, the centre of her cult, where King Attalus of Pergamon, thinking no doubt that the gratitude of Rome was a greater asset than the presence of the goddess, agreed to release the sacred black stone that represented her. She was received at Ostia, the port of Rome, by a welcoming committee that included Scipio and the chief ladies of Rome, who carried her to a temple on the Palatine. Various stories were told of miraculous events signalling her arrival; a new festival of games was inaugurated in her honour and, next year, Hannibal left Italy.

Whether the Romans realized it at the time or not, the worship of Cybele was thoroughly un-Roman. It was violent and orgiastic, and led by eunuch priests who performed frenzied dances, lashing themselves with whips and cutting themselves with knives. The Senate swiftly imposed a ban on Roman citizens participating in these barbarous ceremonies.

Cybele, as the 'Great Mother', was sometimes identified by the Greeks with Rhea, the mother of the gods. She was said to have helped Dionysus after Hera had driven him mad, and her cult was vaguely linked with that of Dionysus, whose origin, of course, was also eastern. In fact, some twenty years after Cybele had been introduced to Rome, there was a troublesome outbreak of Dionysiac worship, the Bacchanalia, probably introduced, like many foreign religions, by prisoners of war. The cult spread alarmingly among the young. According to Livy it concealed aspects far more menacing than drunkenness and sexual promiscuity; it threatened total anarchy and served as a disguise for all kinds of crime. There were rumours of human sacrifices. It was controlled by strict regulations, which did not banish the cult but hedged it in so closely that it was virtually strangled, though it did not die. It was perhaps a sign of the need of ordinary people for something more colourful, more emotional, than the state religion provided, a need implicitly recognized by the authorities when they forebore to outlaw the worship of Bacchus outright.

Like Cybele, the Egyptian goddess Isis was especially attractive to women. Though she never attained the status of the Great Mother, she was worshipped throughout the Roman Empire. Her popularity outside Egypt was largely due to Ptolemy, who consciously encouraged a Hellenized cult of Isis and Osiris as against the old Egyptian gods who, being often in the form of animals, above the shoulders at least, would not have appealed to the Greek mind (in Egypt, Isis was sometimes portrayed with the head of a lioness). The worship of Isis was elegant, with priests swathed in linen, solemn processions, music and incense. She was the wife of Osiris, god of the dead, and the mother of Horus, a sun god. Her myths, which are complex and even more inconsistent than most, are also, naturally, Egyptian, though Hellenized to some degree and retold in romanticized form by writers like Plutarch.

Isis and Osiris, like Zeus and Hera, were sister and brother as well as wife and husband. Another pair of deities, Seth and Nephthys, were sometimes complementary to them and sometimes opposed to them. Osiris, with Isis, once ruled the world benevolently, looking after mankind and teaching him how to grow crops. Seth, his brother (whom Greek writers identified with Typhon, the opponent of Zeus), grew jealous and killed him, chopping up his body into fourteen pieces and scattering the pieces around the world. The grieving Isis (who in this aspect was sometimes identified with Demeter-Ceres in the Graeco-Roman world) would not rest until she had found all the pieces, and she did succeed in reassembling the corpse, except for the genitals. With the aid of other goddesses, she made the body of Osiris into the first mummy.

Below, left:
Cybele enthroned, flanked by lions. The goddess was well known to the Greeks for centuries before the Romans adopted her; her lions were pictured at Delphi taking part in the war between the gods and the giants.

Below:
Attis, Cybele's consort. The priests of Cybele castrated themselves when they vowed their eternal devotion, and that condition is manifested in this marble figure of Attis found in Ostia and now in the Lateran Museum.

A Roman statue of the Egyptian goddess Isis. She carries a sistrum (a kind of rattle) and a jug (a form of cornucopia – she was the eternal Mother-goddess of Egypt) and wears the knot on her breast which represents fertility.

Soon after the death of Osiris, Isis gave birth to a son, Horus, whom she reared secretly in the hope that he would one day overthrow the usurper Seth and avenge his father. When Horus grew up, he fought with Seth and dealt with him as Cronus had dealt with Uranus, though in the fight Horus lost his eye. The other gods interfered to stop the quarrel, Horus was judged to be in the right and received the kingdom of Osiris, who retired to rule the land of the blessed. (In Egypt, Horus represented the living pharaoh while Osiris represented his immortal predecessor in the after-life.)

The gods, in this respect resembling the Olympians – or, indeed, contemporary world leaders – proved to be, in their role of peace-keeping force, well-meaning but impotent; for the conflict between Horus and Seth was renewed. Horus, however, enjoyed the advantage, though it was sometimes a mixed blessing, of his mother's support.

Isis was regarded as omniscient; she had even discovered the ultimate secret – the secret name of Re, king of the gods – which gave her certain universal powers. She had obtained her knowledge by a trick. Having obtained some of Re's spit, she used it to moisten some soil from which she made a snake. She placed the snake where Re would step on it, and it bit him, causing excruciating pain. Isis said she could heal him, but if her magic were to work she would have to know Re's secret name. In agony, Re at last told her, and thus Isis gained powers equal to those of Re himself.

When Isis took her son's part before the tribunal of the gods, Seth was irritated beyond reason, and refused to take any further part in the proceedings unless Isis were barred from them. The tribunal therefore removed to a distant island, and the god of ferries was told not to provide transport for Isis. But she was too clever to be thwarted so easily. She deceived the ferry god by changing into an old woman, and once on the island she changed again, this time to a beautiful young girl. Seth was attracted by her and, having gained his confidence, Isis succeeded in drawing out of him the admission that Horus' claim to rule was better than his own. The gods were forced to admit that Seth had ruined his own cause, and gave Horus the crown.

Seth was not finished yet. He challenged Horus to a contest: which one could stay under water longest before coming up for breath. Taking the form of hippopotami, they plunged beneath the surface, but Isis became alarmed and flung a spear, meaning to hit Seth. Unfortunately she wounded Horus instead, but her second spear hit Seth in the back. Then occurred one of those dramatic and wholly inconsistent events that are rather frequent in myths, which are drawn from multiple sources. Isis took pity on Seth and removed the spear, which made Horus so angry that he cut off his mother's head and carried it away. Seth was sent to bring Horus back, but when he found him he tore out his eyes and placed them on a mountain to bring light to the earth. But they grew into lotus blossoms. Meanwhile, Horus' sight was restored by Hathor, the Cow-goddess.

Above, left:
A head of Mithras from Italy was found in London in 1954, when a complete Mithraeum (temple) was excavated at Walbrook. The head dates from about A.D. 200.

Above:
An alabaster carving from Anatolia of the second century A.D. when the region was part of the Roman empire. It shows the god known as Men, who seems to have been a contrived deity, like Serapis. He has attributes of both Dionysus (the thyrsus in his right hand), and Mithras (the bull on which he places his foot).

Opposite:
The personification of the River Nile, reclining like Jove in a Roman marble sculpture.

187

Isis took firm hold of the Roman imagination, and mystery cults were established at Rome, Pompeii and other places. This Pompeian fresco shows the elegant ritual of Isis worship.

Above, right:
Mithras, as he was seen in the centrepiece of nearly all his temples. The sacrifice of the bull releases life in the form of the animal's blood – an ear of wheat is already forming from his tail. Sun and moon look on, and the earth's creatures come to share in the release of life. Mithras became an immensely popular god among the Roman soldiers.

Various other tricks were attempted by Seth and thwarted by Isis, but the gods, in spite of their confirmation of Horus' rights, were dithering again. Osiris was consulted, and he not surprisingly responded angrily that Horus ought to have been installed long ago. He went on to say that, unless this were done, he would take steps in the matter himself. Frightened by the threats of the god of the dead, the gods again confirmed Horus as king, and this time the decision was final. Seth was sent off to be god of storms, an office in which he could rage against the world as much as he liked.

This story, though an arresting one, of course belongs to Egyptian mythology; though known, at least in part, in the Graeco-Roman world, it had little significance for the Romans.

The most powerful of all the religious cults which came to Rome from the East was Mithraism: it has been said that, if Christianity had never existed, much of the world today would be Mithraist.

Mithras, or Mithra, was an Iranian god. Although relations between the Persian and the Greek worlds were almost invariably hostile for the best part of a thousand years, there was willy-nilly much interaction of the two cultures. The similarities between the Roman Caesars and the old Persian kings, for example, were more than passing. The religion of Mithras became the most widespread, longest lasting and most potent cult in the Roman empire, and was acclaimed by Diocletian as the chief imperial religion, a position from which it was eventually dislodged by Christianity. The discovery of a splendid Mithraic temple in the very centre of London during rebuilding after the blitz of the Second World War was one of the most exciting archaeological finds of recent times, and another sign of the strength of the cult in distant Roman provinces.

The origins of Mithras-worship in Italy are lost in mystery. According to Plutarch, among the earliest worshippers of Mithras were the pirates of Asia Minor whom Pompey captured in 67 B.C. and settled in other parts, including southern Italy. Asia Minor certainly seems to have been the immediate origin of the god. Numerous temples to him were built there during Persian occupation of the region. Mithraism was a disciplined, military religion which placed much emphasis on the virtue of loyalty; it appealed particularly to soldiers, and it was undoubtedly the popularity of Mithras among the legions that produced such substantial signs of his cult in places as far afield as Britain – and at a time, incidentally, when sophisticated Romans had little time for religion of any sort. Mithraism also suited the cult of a divine emperor and thus generally received encouragement from the authorities: Nero tended to identify himself with Mithras. It was not associated with riotous and socially undesirable behaviour of the kind that attended Cybele or Bacchus (the nasty business of baptism in the blood of a slaughtered ox was not originally a Mithraic practice, being borrowed from the Great Mother cult).

From what we know of it, the cosmogony of Mithraism was similar in spirit to the Greek, with successive generations of gods or godlike forces. At the beginning stood Time, who may be the figure often portrayed in art as roughly human but with a lion's head and a snake twined around the body; he carried the keys of heaven, often a thunderbolt too, and was marked with zodiacal signs. (This figure is also identified as Cronus, or as the Persian god Ahriman.) From this *fons et origo* were descended Heaven and Earth and their child Ocean. That is a very Greek conception; but Mithraism differed radically from Greek ideas in positing a force of evil, a darkness inhabited by devils who brought horrors to earth. Against this power stood Mithras, the god of light, whose domain reached from Heaven to Hell.

It was said that Mithras was born at the winter solstice in a cave in the rocks (temples to Mithras – mithraeums – were therefore frequently built underground), and his first worshippers were the shepherds who offered him lambs as sacrifice. In the Roman cult of Mithras, he was represented as a kind of Herculean figure, wearing a Phrygian bonnet and engaged in a number of perilous tasks, like the Labours of Hercules, for the benefit of mankind. The most significant of his exploits, although it is impossible to say why it was so significant, was the slaying of a bull, a scene frequently depicted on Mithraic altars. It probably represents a sacrifice rather than a Herculean-type adventure; myth explained it as an incident in Mithras' contest with the Sun, a trial of strength that ended in an amiable pact, whereupon Mithras sacrificed the bull that he had been set to capture. From its body flowed blessings for mankind.

Mithraism contributed largely to the early Christian heresy of Manichaeanism but, more important, it paved the way for the victory of Christianity in the Roman world by introducing monotheism (one god) and the important moral principle of dualism (Good and Evil). Christianity, however, proved a great deal less welcome in Rome than Mithraism. The early Christians were persecuted not because the authorities disapproved of their doctrines, which were no more objectionable than those of many other cults, but because the Christians themselves were intolerant of all other religions, and attacked them fiercely. Among other objects, their hostility was directed against the concept of the divinity of the emperor, which made them dangerous political opponents of the regime.

The horrors of the gladiatorial arena naturally gained the Roman authorities a very bad reputation with later Christian writers. More recently it has become customary to point out that the Romans were in fact highly tolerant in religious matters and that the early Christians brought martyrdom upon themselves (it has always been rather difficult to regard Pontius Pilate as a villain). In fact, the pendulum may have swung too far: the Roman authorities were tolerant towards new religions as long as they offered no threat to the establishment, but no longer. Even the comparatively harmless cult of Isis provoked partial repression on several occasions.

Nevertheless, Christianity proved victorious in the end, and Christian propagandists zealously set about the demolition of rival beliefs. It was not too difficult to ridicule the goings-on of the Greek gods, and St Augustine, for one, displayed considerable wit in his scornful remarks about the inhabitants of Mount Olympus. Yet they survived to play a part in Western art and literature second only to Christianity itself.

Serapis, often referred to as Zeus-Serapis or Jupiter Apis, was a very strange god indeed, partially invented by King Ptolemy to represent an omnipotent, all-purpose deity – a god for all occasions. His origins have been ascribed to Babylon and to Memphis (the connection there is with the Apis bulls of Egypt). The idea was developed by the Greeks of Alexandria and eventually almost all powers were ascribed to Serapis, including fertility, which is indicated by the *modius* symbol he wears on his head. This bust comes from the Walbrook Mithraeum, London.

Index

Figures in italics refer to illustrations